GUNFIGHTER®

PRECISION RIFLE

WARM UPS, DRILLS, EXERCISES AND QUALS

NAME: _____ UNIT: _____

www.GUNFIGHTERSERIES.com ©

Weapon Conditions

- Condition 4: No mag inserted. Slide/bolt forward on empty chamber. Hammer forward (if applicable). Weapon on safe (if applicable).

- Condition 3: Loaded mag inserted. Slide/bolt forward on empty chamber. Hammer forward (if applicable). Weapon on safe (if applicable).

- Condition 2: Loaded mag inserted. Slide/bolt forward with round in chamber. Hammer forward (if applicable). Weapon on safe (if applicable).

- Condition 1: Loaded mag inserted. Slide/bolt forward with round in chamber. Hammer cocked (if applicable). Weapon on safe (if applicable).

Always know the condition of your weapon!

Safety

- Treat every weapon as if it were loaded.

- Never point your weapon at anything you do not intend to shoot/destroy.

- Know your target and it's background.

- Keep your finger off the trigger until you intend to fire.

- Keep your weapon on safe until you are ready to fire.

- Always wear eye and ear protection, and proper protective clothing.

- Never shoot faster than you can effectively keep rounds on target.

- Be extremely cautious with back splatter and ricochets when shooting steel.

Warning

Perform these drills at your own risk. Only perform these drill in a safe manner which do not violate your range rules. Consult range staff for rules and regulations regarding drawing from a holster, rapid fire and multiple target engagements.

GUNFIGHTER is not responsible for any injury or death that may occur due to the use of this book. We recommend never shooting alone and under supervision of trained safety officers.

Table of Contents:

Admin and Logistics.

Manipulation Drills.
1. Bolt Manipulation
2. Speed Reload

Natural Point Of Aim Drills.
1. NPA
2. Blind Spot
3. Down Up
4. Rapid Bolt Manipulation
5. Speed Dots

Scope Drills
1. Turret Drill
2. Battle Ship
3. Come Up Quick

Accuracy Drills
1. Cold Bore Plus 4
2. Precision Gingy Ninji
3. Know Your Pone Limit
4. Hostage
5. The Recoil Game

Range Estimation Drill

Wind Estimation Drills
1. Wind Arc
2. Wind Reading

Position Drills
1. Sit Kneel Stand (Sling)
2. Sit Kneel Stand (Supported)
3. Dot Torture
4. Prone vs. Positional
5. Threesome
6. Sniper Dice

Multiple Target Drills
1. Lateral Shuffle
2. Head Strong
3. Up And Up

Multiple Target Drills Continued
4. Going the Distance
5. One And Done

Gunfighter Drills
1. Real World Cold Bore
2. Burpee Battle
3. Sniper Prez
4. Assault Course
5. Sniper Sprints
6. Snap Shot
7. Movement To Contac
8. Break Contact

FBI Sniper Qual

Gunfighter PR Standard 1

Custom Drill

Notes Pages

Class Contacts and Notes

Admin & Logistics - 2

Precision Rifle ©

www.GUNFIGHTERSERIES.com ©

How to use this book:

This book offers a carefully crafted catalog of training drills and is designed to log and track training progression as well as shot pattern placement analysis. **All paper targets may be downloaded for free** of our www.GunfighterSereis.com website and printed at home for free with the exception of the JD-QUAL1 target which may be purchased at numerous online retailers. The JD-Qual1 target may also be substituted with a cardboard IPSC with a rectangular body A zone. Some long range drills are designed for instant feedback by using steel targets.

For best results, conduct and record every drill at least once starting at the beginning. The more data you collect the better your results will be.

Most drills offer defensive time and scoring goals to achieve. Competitive shooters may set different goals and use special competition rules. Everyone's goal should be to improve their recorded personal best.

For proper weapons handling and marksmanship coaching, seek out well respected firearms instructors and courses.

Train safe. Train hard. Train to win.

Afterwards:

Upon mastering all the drills in this book, continue to increase your skills by utilizing the entire Gunfighter training log book series.

Gunfighter Skill Books 2016 © - Gunfighter, LLC - All Rights Reserved

ISBN: 9781702229852   Revised 2020

Round Count Log

Weapon Make & Model: **SN#:**

Date	Ammo	Lot #	Fired	Total

Date	Ammo	Lot #	Fired	Total

This Page	
Previous Page	
TOTAL	

Notes:

Admin & Logistics - 4

Precision Rifle ©

Round Count Log

www.GUNFIGHTERSERIES.com ©

Weapon Make & Model:

SN#:

Date	Ammo	Lot #	Fired	Total

Date	Ammo	Lot #	Fired	Total

This Page
Previous Page
TOTAL

Notes:

Round Count Log

Weapon Make & Model: SN#:

Date	Ammo	Lot #	Fired	Total

Date	Ammo	Lot #	Fired	Total

This Page	
Previous Page	
TOTAL	

Notes:

Admin & Logistics - 4

Round Count Log

www.GUNFIGHTERSERIES.com ©

Weapon Make & Model:

SN#:

Date	Ammo	Lot #	Fired	Total	Date	Ammo	Lot #	Fired	Total

This Page	
Previous Page	
TOTAL	

Notes:

Maintenance Log

Weapon Make & Model: SN#:

Date	Full Cleaning	Damage Inspection	Date	Full Cleaning	Damage Inspection
	Y / N	Y / N		Y / N	Y / N
	Y / N	Y / N		Y / N	Y / N
	Y / N	Y / N		Y / N	Y / N
	Y / N	Y / N		Y / N	Y / N
	Y / N	Y / N		Y / N	Y / N
	Y / N	Y / N		Y / N	Y / N
	Y / N	Y / N		Y / N	Y / N
	Y / N	Y / N		Y / N	Y / N
	Y / N	Y / N		Y / N	Y / N
	Y / N	Y / N		Y / N	Y / N
	Y / N	Y / N		Y / N	Y / N
	Y / N	Y / N		Y / N	Y / N
	Y / N	Y / N		Y / N	Y / N
	Y / N	Y / N		Y / N	Y / N

Parts Replaced:

Notes:

RIFLE SET UP

Purpose: To ensure the rifle system is married to your body.

Distance: 1 - 2 inches.

Target: Blank white wall.

Extra Equipment Needed: Scope and rifle tools.

Total Rounds Fired: 0 Rounds

Starting Position & Condition: Prone position. Condition 4.

Comb Height: Assume a good prone position resting your cheek naturally and comfortably on the stock of your rifle. Most shooters will need to raise the comb height to compensate for larger scopes to achieve good sight picture. This can be done with adjustable stocks or by simply duct taping foam pad to your stock. Have your spotter look through the objective lens to ensure the reticle is bisecting your pupil.

Sight Picture: Assume a good prone position with your rifle muzzle inches from a blank white wall/paper. Being completely relaxed, look through your scope observing the edges of the picture for crispness. You may need to loosen your rings, adjust your scope eye relief forward or backward until there is absolutely no shadow, level scope with rifle then tighten rings to recommended torque setting.

Reticle Clarity: Assume a good prone position with your rifle muzzle inches from a blank white wall/paper. Being completely relaxed with your eyes closed, open your eyes and quickly check for reticle clarity. Must be quick, because your eye will naturally focus if reticle is not crisp. Repeat closing your eyes several time while making bold adjustments to the ocular lens until the reticle is instantly clear. Readjust after every trip to the optometrist.

* These procedures should be done in summer and winter to adjust for bulky winter clothing and possible winter holiday weight gains.

RIFLE SET UP

Rifle: Scope:

Date	Winter / Summer	Comb, Sight Pic, Reticle Check	Any Changes:
		Y / N	
		Y / N	
		Y / N	
		Y / N	
		Y / N	
		Y / N	
		Y / N	
		Y / N	
		Y / N	
		Y / N	
		Y / N	
		Y / N	
		Y / N	
		Y / N	
		Y / N	
		Y / N	
		Y / N	
		Y / N	
		Y / N	

RIFLE SET UP

www.GUNFIGHTERSERIES.com ©

Rifle: Scope:

Date	Winter / Summer	Comb, Sight Pic, Reticle Check	Any Changes:
		Y / N	
		Y / N	
		Y / N	
		Y / N	
		Y / N	
		Y / N	
		Y / N	
		Y / N	
		Y / N	
		Y / N	
		Y / N	
		Y / N	
		Y / N	
		Y / N	
		Y / N	
		Y / N	

RIFLE SET UP

Rifle: Scope:

Date	Winter / Summer	Comb, Sight Pic, Reticle Check	Any Changes:
		Y / N	
		Y / N	
		Y / N	
		Y / N	
		Y / N	
		Y / N	
		Y / N	
		Y / N	
		Y / N	
		Y / N	
		Y / N	
		Y / N	
		Y / N	
		Y / N	
		Y / N	
		Y / N	
		Y / N	

BOLT MANIPULATION (Bolt Action Rifles)

Purpose: To develop consistent trigger control, sight picture, follow through and body position.

Distance: 1 - 2 inches.

Target: Blank white wall.

Total Rounds Fired: 0 Rounds.

Repetitions: 10 Reps.

Starting Position & Condition: Prone position. Condition 4.

Description: Assume a good prone position with your rifle muzzle inches from a blank white wall/paper. Be sure you are in condition 4 with no ammo in magazine. Take your rifle off safe, squeeze the trigger without disturbing your NPA (Natural Point of Aim). Keeping your cheek welded to the stock with a clear sight picture, avoiding any unnecessary movement causing you to shift sight alignment, with your firing hand unlock and slide the bolt to the rear. While still maintain a clear sight picture slide the bolt forward to the locking position. Repeat 9 more times.

Goals: Be smooth and deliberate while decreasing your time to fully cycle the bolt.

BOLT MANIPULATION

Date:	Location:	Weapon:	10 Reps?	Notes:
			Y / N	
			Y / N	
			Y / N	
			Y / N	
			Y / N	
			Y / N	
			Y / N	
			Y / N	
			Y / N	
			Y / N	
			Y / N	
			Y / N	
			Y / N	
			Y / N	
			Y / N	
			Y / N	
			Y / N	
			Y / N	

Manipulation Drill - 1

Precision Rifle ©

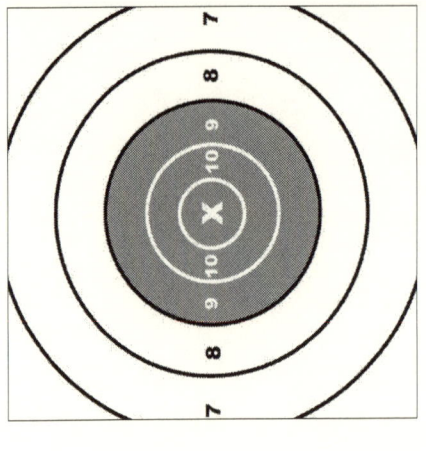

SPEED RELOAD

Purpose: To increase reloading time with external box magazines and gear placement familiarization.

Distance: 25 Yards.

Target: GF-2

Par Time: 10 Seconds.

Extra Equipment Needed: Shot timer. 2 Mags; 1 with 0 rounds, 1 with 1 round. Mag pouch.

Rounds Fired Per Rep: 3 Rounds.   **Total Rounds Fired:** 9 Rounds.

Point Penalty: As per target score.

Repetitions: 3 Reps.

Description (DRY): Assume a good shooting position with a condition 3 rifle - no rounds in mag. (Lock bolt to the rear for semi-auto rifles.) Aim in and dry fire. Drop magazine in place, reload, send bolt forward and dry fire again. Conduct 10 reps in the prone, kneeling and standing positions.

Description (LIVE): Assume a good shooting position with a condition 3 rifle - no rounds in mag. (Lock bolt to the rear for semi-auto rifles.) At the timer beep, aim in and dry fire. Drop magazine in place, reload with a mag of 1 round, send bolt forward and fire 1 round in a time limit of 10 seconds. Conduct 3 reps in the prone, kneeling and standing positions recording your fastest time. For tightest groups; take a little extra time before the buzzer beep to ensure your body position and NPA are correct.

Goals: Beat your personal best score.

Variations: Lower par time to 8 seconds. To add more emphasis on accuracy move target to 100 yards.

Speed Reload

Date:	Rifle:	Scope:	Distance: 25 Y / 100 Y
1st Prone Time:	1st Kneeling Time:	1st Standing Time:	Dry Fire Each X 10: Y / N
2nd Prone Time:	2nd Kneeling Time:	2nd Standing Time:	Notes:
3rd Prone Time:	3rd Kneeling Time:	3rd Standing Time:	
Best Prone Time:	Best Kneeling Time:	Best Standing Time:	
Prone Score:	Kneeling Score:	Standing Score:	Score: # of X's:
Date:	Rifle:	Scope:	Distance: 25 Y / 100 Y
1st Prone Time:	1st Kneeling Time:	1st Standing Time:	Dry Fire Each X 10: Y / N
2nd Prone Time:	2nd Kneeling Time:	2nd Standing Time:	Notes:
3rd Prone Time:	3rd Kneeling Time	3rd Standing Time:	
Best Prone Time:	Best Kneeling Time:	Best Standing Time:	
Prone Score:	Kneeling Score:	Standing Score:	Score: # of X's:
Date:	Rifle:	Scope:	Distance: 25 Y / 100 Y
1st Prone Time:	1st Kneeling Time:	1st Standing Time:	Dry Fire Each X 10: Y / N
2nd Prone Time:	2nd Kneeling Time:	2nd Standing Time:	Notes:
3rd Prone Time:	3rd Kneeling Time:	3rd Standing Time:	
Best Prone Time:	Best Kneeling Time:	Best Standing Time:	
Prone Score:	Kneeling Score:	Standing Score:	Score: # of X's:

Manipulation Drill - 2

Speed Reload

Date:	Rifle:	Scope:	Distance: 25 Y / 100 Y
1st Prone Time:	1st Kneeling Time:	1st Standing Time:	Dry Fire Each X 10: Y / N
2nd Prone Time:	2nd Kneeling Time:	2nd Standing Time:	Notes:
3rd Prone Time:	3rd Kneeling Time:	3rd Standing Time:	
Best Prone Time:	Best Kneeling Time:	Best Standing Time:	
Prone Score:	Kneeling Score:	Standing Score:	Score: # of X's:
Date:	Rifle:	Scope:	Distance: 25 Y / 100 Y
1st Prone Time:	1st Kneeling Time:	1st Standing Time:	Dry Fire Each X 10: Y / N
2nd Prone Time:	2nd Kneeling Time:	2nd Standing Time:	Notes:
3rd Prone Time:	3rd Kneeling Time:	3rd Standing Time:	
Best Prone Time:	Best Kneeling Time:	Best Standing Time:	
Prone Score:	Kneeling Score:	Standing Score:	Score: # of X's:
Date:	Rifle:	Scope:	Distance: 25 Y / 100 Y
1st Prone Time:	1st Kneeling Time:	1st Standing Time:	Dry Fire Each X 10: Y / N
2nd Prone Time:	2nd Kneeling Time:	2nd Standing Time:	Notes:
3rd Prone Time:	3rd Kneeling Time:	3rd Standing Time:	
Best Prone Time:	Best Kneeling Time:	Best Standing Time:	
Prone Score:	Kneeling Score:	Standing Score:	Score: # of X's:

Speed Reload

Date:	Rifle:	Scope:	Distance: 25 Y / 100 Y
1st Prone Time:	1st Kneeling Time:	1st Standing Time:	Dry Fire Each X 10: Y / N
2nd Prone Time:	2nd Kneeling Time:	2nd Standing Time:	Notes:
3rd Prone Time:	3rd Kneeling Time:	3rd Standing Time:	
Best Prone Time:	Best Kneeling Time:	Best Standing Time:	
Prone Score:	Kneeling Score:	Standing Score:	Score: # of X's:
Date:	Rifle:	Scope:	Distance: 25 Y / 100 Y
1st Prone Time:	1st Kneeling Time:	1st Standing Time:	Dry Fire Each X 10: Y / N
2nd Prone Time:	2nd Kneeling Time:	2nd Standing Time:	Notes:
3rd Prone Time:	3rd Kneeling Time:	3rd Standing Time:	
Best Prone Time:	Best Kneeling Time:	Best Standing Time:	
Prone Score:	Kneeling Score:	Standing Score:	Score: # of X's:
Date:	Rifle:	Scope:	Distance: 25 Y / 100 Y
1st Prone Time:	1st Kneeling Time:	1st Standing Time:	Dry Fire Each X 10: Y / N
2nd Prone Time:	2nd Kneeling Time:	2nd Standing Time:	Notes:
3rd Prone Time:	3rd Kneeling Time:	3rd Standing Time:	
Best Prone Time:	Best Kneeling Time:	Best Standing Time:	
Prone Score:	Kneeling Score:	Standing Score:	Score: # of X's:

Manipulation Drill - 2

Precision Rifle ©

Speed Reload

Date:	Rifle:	Scope:	Distance: 25 Y / 100 Y
1st Prone Time:	1st Kneeling Time:	1st Standing Time:	Dry Fire Each X 10: Y / N
2nd Prone Time:	2nd Kneeling Time:	2nd Standing Time:	Notes:
3rd Prone Time:	3rd Kneeling Time:	3rd Standing Time:	
Best Prone Time:	Best Kneeling Time:	Best Standing Time:	
Prone Score:	**Kneeling Score:**	**Standing Score:**	**Score:** # of X's:
Date:	Rifle:	Scope:	Distance: 25 Y / 100 Y
1st Prone Time:	1st Kneeling Time:	1st Standing Time:	Dry Fire Each X 10: Y / N
2nd Prone Time:	2nd Kneeling Time:	2nd Standing Time:	Notes:
3rd Prone Time:	3rd Kneeling Time:	3rd Standing Time:	
Best Prone Time:	Best Kneeling Time:	Best Standing Time:	
Prone Score:	**Kneeling Score:**	**Standing Score:**	**Score:** # of X's:
Date:	Rifle:	Scope:	Distance: 25 Y / 100 Y
1st Prone Time:	1st Kneeling Time:	1st Standing Time:	Dry Fire Each X 10: Y / N
2nd Prone Time:	2nd Kneeling Time:	2nd Standing Time:	Notes:
3rd Prone Time:	3rd Kneeling Time:	3rd Standing Time:	
Best Prone Time:	Best Kneeling Time:	Best Standing Time:	
Prone Score:	**Kneeling Score:**	**Standing Score:**	**Score:** # of X's:

Speed Reload

Manipulation Drill - 2

Date:	Rifle:	Scope:	Distance: 25 Y / 100 Y
1st Prone Time:	1st Kneeling Time	1st Standing Time:	Dry Fire Each X 10: Y / N
2nd Prone Time:	2nd Kneeling Time:	2nd Standing Time:	Notes:
3rd Prone Time:	3rd Kneeling Time:	3rd Standing Time:	
Best Prone Time:	Best Kneeling Time:	Best Standing Time:	
Prone Score:	Kneeling Score:	Standing Score:	Score: # of X's:
Date:	Rifle:	Scope:	Distance: 25 Y / 100 Y
1st Prone Time:	1st Kneeling Time:	1st Standing Time:	Dry Fire Each X 10: Y / N
2nd Prone Time:	2nd Kneeling Time:	2nd Standing Time:	Notes:
3rd Prone Time:	3rd Kneeling Time:	3rd Standing Time:	
Best Prone Time:	Best Kneeling Time:	Best Standing Time:	
Prone Score:	Kneeling Score:	Standing Score:	Score: # of X's:
Date:	Rifle:	Scope:	Distance: 25 Y / 100 Y
1st Prone Time:	1st Kneeling Time:	1st Standing Time:	Dry Fire Each X 10: Y / N
2nd Prone Time:	2nd Kneeling Time:	2nd Standing Time:	Notes:
3rd Prone Time:	3rd Kneeling Time:	3rd Standing Time:	
Best Prone Time:	Best Kneeling Time:	Best Standing Time:	
Prone Score:	Kneeling Score:	Standing Score:	Score: # of X's:

Precision Rifle ©

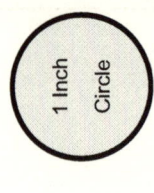

1 Inch Circle

NATURAL POINT OF AIM

Purpose: Establishing a solid shooting position.

Distance: 100 Yards.

Target: 1 inch circle or square.

Total Rounds Fired: 0 Rounds.

Repetitions: 4 Reps.

Starting Position & Condition: Prone. Condition 4.

Description: Position rifle pointing at the target. Assume a good prone position with front and rear support. Adjust parallax until the target picture is equally clear as the reticle. Test by slightly shaking your head left / right and up /down. The reticle should not drift off target.

Once you are in position. Close your eyes, take a deep breath and release then open your eyes. Reticle should be on target. If you are off target adjust your entire body position, do not muscle the reticle into place which will cause tension and a point of aim—point of impact shift. Close your eyes, deep breathing cycle then open eyes to confirm NPA (Natural Point of Aim).

Do this NPA test every time you break from a shooting position. Check parallax every time you change target distances.

Goals: Zero movement with deep breathing cycle.

Variations: Try doing this NPA test in the prone, sitting, kneeling and standing. Have a coach simulate recoil by pushing your muzzle.

www.gunfighterseries.com ©

NPA Test

Date:	Rifle:	Parallax	Prone	Sitting	Kneeling	Prone	Notes:
		Y / N	Y / N	Y / N	Y / N	Y / N	
		Y / N	Y / N	Y / N	Y / N	Y / N	
		Y / N	Y / N	Y / N	Y / N	Y / N	
		Y / N	Y / N	Y / N	Y / N	Y / N	
		Y / N	Y / N	Y / N	Y / N	Y / N	
		Y / N	Y / N	Y / N	Y / N	Y / N	
		Y / N	Y / N	Y / N	Y / N	Y / N	
		Y / N	Y / N	Y / N	Y / N	Y / N	
		Y / N	Y / N	Y / N	Y / N	Y / N	
		Y / N	Y / N	Y / N	Y / N	Y / N	
		Y / N	Y / N	Y / N	Y / N	Y / N	
		Y / N	Y / N	Y / N	Y / N	Y / N	
		Y / N	Y / N	Y / N	Y / N	Y / N	
		Y / N	Y / N	Y / N	Y / N	Y / N	
		Y / N	Y / N	Y / N	Y / N	Y / N	
		Y / N	Y / N	Y / N	Y / N	Y / N	
		Y / N	Y / N	Y / N	Y / N	Y / N	
		Y / N	Y / N	Y / N	Y / N	Y / N	

N.P.A. Drill - 1

BLIND SPOT

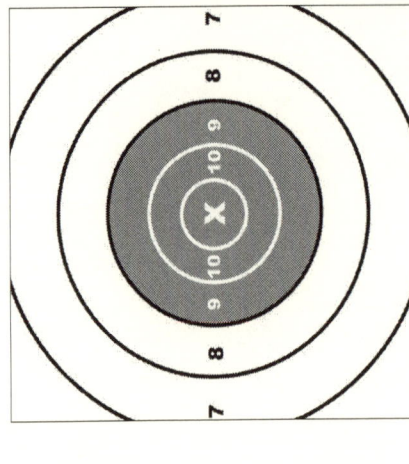

Purpose: Natural Point of Aim practice and verification.

Distance: 100 Yards. **Target:** GF-2

Extra Equipment Needed: Spotting scope, piece of cardboard and shooting partner.

Rounds Fired Per Rep: 1 Round. **Total Rounds Fired:** 5 Rounds.

Repetitions: 5 Reps.

Starting Position & Condition: Prone. Condition 1. Scope on personal rifle ZERO.

Note: This drill should only be done with a competent shooting partner and controlled by range safety supervision with extreme caution.

Description: Position rifle pointing at the target. Assume a good prone position with front and rear support. Adjust parallax until the target picture is equally clear as the reticle. Test parallax by slightly shaking your head left / right and up /down. The reticle should not drift off target. Once you are in a solid supported position. Close your eyes, take a deep breath inhaling, exhaling then open your eyes. The reticle should be quartering target. If you are off target adjust your entire body position, do not muscle the reticle into place which will cause tension and a point of aim—point of impact shift. Repeat this process several times.

When you are certain your natural point of aim is correct and you are ready to fire, have your spotter place a barrier (paper or cardboard) in front of your scope's objective lens. Fire 1 round blind. If your natural point of aim is true and you haven't moved the rifle, your round will impact in the center of the target verifying your natural point of aim. Repeat deep breathing cycle several times between the 5 live shots.

Goals: 50 Points with 5 X's. The more stable your position and more relaxed you are during breathing cycle, the tighter your groups will be.

Variation: Block the view, do a deep breathing cycle while blind, then fire 1 round while blind to test your bodies NPA position.

BLIND SPOT

Date:	Rifle:	Scope:	Ammo:	Notes:
Elev: Wind:	Support Type:		Score: # of X's:	

Date:	Rifle:	Scope:	Ammo:	Notes:
Elev: Wind:	Support Type:		Score: # of X's:	

Date:	Rifle:	Scope:	Ammo:	Notes:
Elev: Wind:	Support Type:		Score: # of X's:	

Date:	Rifle:	Scope:	Ammo:	Notes:
Elev: Wind:	Support Type:		Score: # of X's:	

Date:	Rifle:	Scope:	Ammo:	Notes:
Elev: Wind:	Support Type:		Score: # of X's:	

N.P.A. Drill - 2

Precision Rifle ©

BLIND SPOT

Date:	Rifle:	Scope:	Ammo:	Notes:
Elev: Wind:	Support Type:		**Score:** **# of X's:**	

Date:	Rifle:	Scope:	Ammo:	Notes:
Elev: Wind:	Support Type:		**Score:** **# of X's:**	

Date:	Rifle:	Scope:	Ammo:	Notes:
Elev: Wind:	Support Type:		**Score:** **# of X's:**	

Date:	Rifle:	Scope:	Ammo:	Notes:
Elev: Wind:	Support Type:		**Score:** **# of X's:**	

Date:	Rifle:	Scope:	Ammo:	Notes:
Elev: Wind:	Support Type:		**Score:** **# of X's:**	

www.GUNFIGHTERSERIES.com ©

BLIND SPOT

Date:	Rifle:	Scope:	Ammo:	Notes:
Elev: Wind:	Support Type:	**Score:**	# of X's:	

Date:	Rifle:	Scope:	Ammo:	Notes:
Elev: Wind:	Support Type:	**Score:**	# of X's:	

Date:	Rifle:	Scope:	Ammo:	Notes:
Elev: Wind:	Support Type:	**Score:**	# of X's:	

Date:	Rifle:	Scope:	Ammo:	Notes:
Elev: Wind:	Support Type:	**Score:**	# of X's:	

Date:	Rifle:	Scope:	Ammo:	Notes:
Elev: Wind:	Support Type:	**Score:**	# of X's:	

N.P.A. Drill - 2

BLIND SPOT

www.GUNFIGHTERSERIES.com ©

Date:	Rifle:	Scope:	Ammo:	Notes:
Elev:	Wind:	Support Type:	Score:	# of X's:

Date:	Rifle:	Scope:	Ammo:	Notes:
Elev:	Wind:	Support Type:	Score:	# of X's:

Date:	Rifle:	Scope:	Ammo:	Notes:
Elev:	Wind:	Support Type:	Score:	# of X's:

Date:	Rifle:	Scope:	Ammo:	Notes:
Elev:	Wind:	Support Type:	Score:	# of X's:

Date:	Rifle:	Scope:	Ammo:	Notes:
Elev:	Wind:	Support Type:	Score:	# of X's:

BLIND SPOT

Date:	Rifle:	Scope:	Ammo:	Notes:
Elev:	Wind:	Support Type:		
			Score:	**# of X's:**

Date:	Rifle:	Scope:	Ammo:	Notes:
Elev:	Wind:	Support Type:		
			Score:	**# of X's:**

Date:	Rifle:	Scope:	Ammo:	Notes:
Elev:	Wind:	Support Type:		
			Score:	**# of X's:**

Date:	Rifle:	Scope:	Ammo:	Notes:
Elev:	Wind:	Support Type:		
			Score:	**# of X's:**

Date:	Rifle:	Scope:	Ammo:	Notes:
Elev:	Wind:	Support Type:		
			Score:	**# of X's:**

N.P.A. Drill - 2

DOWN UP

Purpose: To quickly establish a solid prone position, good NPA and proper follow through.

Distance: 100 Yards.

Target: 1 inch dots X 5.

Extra Equipment Needed: Shot timer.

Rounds Fired Per Stage: 2 Rounds.   **Total Rounds Fired:** 10 Rounds.

Point Penalty: Go / No Go (2 Rounds must be in or touching the circle to pass.)

Repetitions: 1 Rep of 5 stages.

Starting Position & Condition: Standing 10 feet behind your rifle. Condition 4.

Description: Place rifle and equipment on the firing line. Place 10 rounds 10+ feet behind the firing line.

At the timer beep, grab 2 rounds, assume a good prone shooting position, load and fire 2 rounds into the first dot. Put weapon in condition 4, stand, retrieve 2 more rounds, assume a good prone position, load and fire 2 rounds into the second dot. Continue this drill for all 5 dots. Try both domanant side and support side shoulders.

Dominant Side Goals: Novice: All hits in dot under 6 minutes.   Expert: All hits in dot under 3 minutes.   Gunfighter: All hits in dot under 2 min.

Support Side Goals: Novice: All hits in dot under 9 minutes.   Expert: All hits in dot under 5 minutes.   Gunfighter: All hits in dot under 3 min.

Variation: Increase distance or use smaller dots.

DOWN UP

Date:	Rifle:	Temp:	Elev: Wind:	Distance:	Dominant / Support Side
Dot 1: Go / No Go	Dot 2: Go / No Go	Dot 3: Go / No Go	Dot 4: Go / No Go	Dot 5: Go / No Go	Final Time:
○	○	○	○	○	Notes:
Date:	Rifle:	Temp:	Elev: Wind:	Distance:	Dominant / Support Side
Dot 1: Go / No Go	Dot 2: Go / No Go	Dot 3: Go / No Go	Dot 4: Go / No Go	Dot 5: Go / No Go	Final Time:
●	●	●	●	●	Notes:
Date:	Rifle:	Temp:	Elev: Wind:	Distance:	Dominant / Support Side
Dot 1: Go / No Go	Dot 2: Go / No Go	Dot 3: Go / No Go	Dot 4: Go / No Go	Dot 5: Go / No Go	Final Time:
○	○	○	○	○	Notes:
Date:	Rifle:	Temp:	Elev: Wind:	Distance:	Dominant / Support Side
Dot 1: Go / No Go	Dot 2: Go / No Go	Dot 3: Go / No Go	Dot 4: Go / No Go	Dot 5: Go / No Go	Final Time:
●	●	●	●	●	Notes:

N.P.A. Drill - 3

Precision Rifle ©

DOWN UP

www.GUNFIGHTERSERIES.com ©

Date:	Rifle:	Temp:	Elev: Wind:	Distance:	Dominant / Support Side
Dot 1: Go / No Go ○	Dot 2: Go / No Go ○	Dot 3: Go / No Go ○	Dot 4: Go / No Go ○	Dot 5: Go / No Go ○	Final Time:
					Notes:
Date:	Rifle:	Temp:	Elev: Wind:	Distance:	Dominant / Support Side
Dot 1: Go / No Go ●	Dot 2: Go / No Go ●	Dot 3: Go / No Go ●	Dot 4: Go / No Go ●	Dot 5: Go / No Go ●	Final Time:
					Notes:
Date:	Rifle:	Temp:	Elev: Wind:	Distance:	Dominant / Support Side
Dot 1: Go / No Go ○	Dot 2: Go / No Go ○	Dot 3: Go / No Go ○	Dot 4: Go / No Go ○	Dot 5: Go / No Go ○	Final Time:
					Notes:
Date:	Rifle:	Temp:	Elev: Wind:	Distance:	Dominant / Support Side
Dot 1: Go / No Go ●	Dot 2: Go / No Go ●	Dot 3: Go / No Go ●	Dot 4: Go / No Go ●	Dot 5: Go / No Go ●	Final Time:
					Notes:

DOWN UP

Date:	Rifle:	Temp:	Elev: Wind:	Distance:	Dominant / Support Side
Dot 1: Go / No Go	Dot 2: Go / No Go	Dot 3: Go / No Go	Dot 4: Go / No Go	Dot 5: Go / No Go	Final Time:
◯	◯	◯	◯	◯	Notes:

Date:	Rifle:	Temp:	Elev: Wind:	Distance:	Dominant / Support Side
Dot 1: Go / No Go	Dot 2: Go / No Go	Dot 3: Go / No Go	Dot 4: Go / No Go	Dot 5: Go / No Go	Final Time:
●	●	●	●	●	Notes:

Date:	Rifle:	Temp:	Elev: Wind:	Distance:	Dominant / Support Side
Dot 1: Go / No Go	Dot 2: Go / No Go	Dot 3: Go / No Go	Dot 4: Go / No Go	Dot 5: Go / No Go	Final Time:
◯	◯	◯	◯	◯	Notes:

Date:	Rifle:	Temp:	Elev: Wind:	Distance:	Dominant / Support Side
Dot 1: Go / No Go	Dot 2: Go / No Go	Dot 3: Go / No Go	Dot 4: Go / No Go	Dot 5: Go / No Go	Final Time:
●	●	●	●	●	Notes:

N.P.A. Drill - 3

Precision Rifle ©

DOWN UP

Date:	Rifle:	Temp:	Elev: Wind:	Distance:	Dominant / Support Side
Dot 1: Go / No Go	Dot 2: Go / No Go	Dot 3: Go / No Go	Dot 4: Go / No Go	Dot 5: Go / No Go	Final Time:
○	○	○	○	○	Notes:
Date:	Rifle:	Temp:	Elev: Wind:	Distance:	Dominant / Support Side
Dot 1: Go / No Go	Dot 2: Go / No Go	Dot 3: Go / No Go	Dot 4: Go / No Go	Dot 5: Go / No Go	Final Time:
●	●	●	●	●	Notes:
Date:	Rifle:	Temp:	Elev: Wind:	Distance:	Dominant / Support Side
Dot 1: Go / No Go	Dot 2: Go / No Go	Dot 3: Go / No Go	Dot 4: Go / No Go	Dot 5: Go / No Go	Final Time:
○	○	○	○	○	Notes:
Date:	Rifle:	Temp:	Elev: Wind:	Distance:	Dominant / Support Side
Dot 1: Go / No Go	Dot 2: Go / No Go	Dot 3: Go / No Go	Dot 4: Go / No Go	Dot 5: Go / No Go	Final Time:
●	●	●	●	●	Notes:

www.GUNFIGHTERSERIES.com ©

DOWN UP

Date:	Rifle:	Temp:	Elev: Wind:	Distance:	Dominant / Support Side
Dot 1: Go / No Go	Dot 2: Go / No Go	Dot 3: Go / No Go	Dot 4: Go / No Go	Dot 5: Go / No Go	Final Time:
○	○	○	○	○	Notes:
Date:	Rifle:	Temp:	Elev: Wind:	Distance:	Dominant / Support Side
Dot 1: Go / No Go	Dot 2: Go / No Go	Dot 3: Go / No Go	Dot 4: Go / No Go	Dot 5: Go / No Go	Final Time:
●	●	●	●	●	Notes:
Date:	Rifle:	Temp:	Elev: Wind:	Distance:	Dominant / Support Side
Dot 1: Go / No Go	Dot 2: Go / No Go	Dot 3: Go / No Go	Dot 4: Go / No Go	Dot 5: Go / No Go	Final Time:
○	○	○	○	○	Notes:
Date:	Rifle:	Temp:	Elev: Wind:	Distance:	Dominant / Support Side
Dot 1: Go / No Go	Dot 2: Go / No Go	Dot 3: Go / No Go	Dot 4: Go / No Go	Dot 5: Go / No Go	Final Time:
●	●	●	●	●	Notes:

N.P.A. Drill - 3

Precision Rifle ©

RAPID BOLT MANIPULATION

Purpose: To reinforce solid shooting position, NPA and follow through.

Distance: 100 Yards.

Target: GF-2

Par Time: 25 Seconds.

Extra Equipment Needed: Shot timer.

Total Rounds Fired: 5 Rounds.

Point Penalty: As per target score.

Repetitions: 1 Rep.

Starting Position & Condition: See description.

Description (DRY): Assume a good prone position with a condition 4 rifle. Conduct a set of 10 dry fires as fast as possible while maintaining perfect sight alignment and sight picture.

Description (LIVE): Place your rifle on the firing ling in condition 1 then stand behind your rifle. At the timer beep, assume a good prone shooting position then fire 5 rounds at the target. For tightest groups; take a little extra time to ensure your body position and NPA are correct.

Goals: Novice: 45 points under par.   Expert: 50 points under par.   Gunfighter: 50 points with 5 X's under par.

Variations: Try at 200 yards with same par time.

RAPID BOLT MANIPULATION

Date:	Rifle:	Scope:	Elev:	Wind:	Notes:
100 yards / 200 yards	Dry Fire X 10: Y / N	Time:	**Score:**	**# of X's:**	

Date:	Rifle:	Scope:	Elev:	Wind:	Notes:
100 yards / 200 yards	Dry Fire X 10: Y / N	Time:	**Score:**	**# of X's:**	

Date:	Rifle:	Scope:	Elev:	Wind:	Notes:
100 yards / 200 yards	Dry Fire X 10: Y / N	Time:	**Score:**	**# of X's:**	

Date:	Rifle:	Scope:	Elev:	Wind:	Notes:
100 yards / 200 yards	Dry Fire X 10: Y / N	Time:	**Score:**	**# of X's:**	

Date:	Rifle:	Scope:	Elev:	Wind:	Notes:
100 yards / 200 yards	Dry Fire X 10: Y / N	Time:	**Score:**	**# of X's:**	

N.P.A. Drill - 4

RAPID BOLT MANIPULATION

Date:	Rifle:	Scope:	Elev:	Wind:	Notes:
100 yards / 200 yards	Dry Fire X 10: Y / N	Time:	**Score:**	**# of X's:**	

Date:	Rifle:	Scope:	Elev:	Wind:	Notes:
100 yards / 200 yards	Dry Fire X 10: Y / N	Time:	**Score:**	**# of X's:**	

Date:	Rifle:	Scope:	Elev:	Wind:	Notes:
100 yards / 200 yards	Dry Fire X 10: Y / N	Time:	**Score:**	**# of X's:**	

Date:	Rifle:	Scope:	Elev:	Wind:	Notes:
100 yards / 200 yards	Dry Fire X 10: Y / N	Time:	**Score:**	**# of X's:**	

Date:	Rifle:	Scope:	Elev:	Wind:	Notes:
100 yards / 200 yards	Dry Fire X 10: Y / N	Time:	**Score:**	**# of X's:**	

www.GUNFIGHTERSERIES.com ©

RAPID BOLT MANIPULATION

Date:	Rifle:	Scope:	Elev:	Wind:	Notes:
100 yards / 200 yards	Dry Fire X 10: Y / N	Time:	**Score:**	**# of X's:**	

Date:	Rifle:	Scope:	Elev:	Wind:	Notes:
100 yards / 200 yards	Dry Fire X 10: Y / N	Time:	**Score:**	**# of X's:**	

Date:	Rifle:	Scope:	Elev:	Wind:	Notes:
100 yards / 200 yards	Dry Fire X 10: Y / N	Time:	**Score:**	**# of X's:**	

Date:	Rifle:	Scope:	Elev:	Wind:	Notes:
100 yards / 200 yards	Dry Fire X 10: Y / N	Time:	**Score:**	**# of X's:**	

Date:	Rifle:	Scope:	Elev:	Wind:	Notes:
100 yards / 200 yards	Dry Fire X 10: Y / N	Time:	**Score:**	**# of X's:**	

N.P.A. Drill - 4

Precision Rifle ©

RAPID BOLT MANIPULATION

Date:	Rifle:	Scope:	Elev:	Wind:	Notes:
100 yards / 200 yards	Dry Fire X 10: Y / N	Time:	**Score:**	**# of X's:**	

Date:	Rifle:	Scope:	Elev:	Wind:	Notes:
100 yards / 200 yards	Dry Fire X 10: Y / N	Time:	**Score:**	**# of X's:**	

Date:	Rifle:	Scope:	Elev:	Wind:	Notes:
100 yards / 200 yards	Dry Fire X 10: Y / N	Time:	**Score:**	**# of X's:**	

Date:	Rifle:	Scope:	Elev:	Wind:	Notes:
100 yards / 200 yards	Dry Fire X 10: Y / N	Time:	**Score:**	**# of X's:**	

Date:	Rifle:	Scope:	Elev:	Wind:	Notes:
100 yards / 200 yards	Dry Fire X 10: Y / N	Time:	**Score:**	**# of X's:**	

www.GUNFIGHTERSERIES.com ©

RAPID BOLT MANIPULATION

Date:	Rifle:	Scope:	Elev:	Wind:	Notes:
100 yards / 200 yards	Dry Fire X 10: Y / N	Time:	**Score:**	**# of X's:**	

Date:	Rifle:	Scope:	Elev:	Wind:	Notes:
100 yards / 200 yards	Dry Fire X 10: Y / N	Time:	**Score:**	**# of X's:**	

Date:	Rifle:	Scope:	Elev:	Wind:	Notes:
100 yards / 200 yards	Dry Fire X 10: Y / N	Time:	**Score:**	**# of X's:**	

Date:	Rifle:	Scope:	Elev:	Wind:	Notes:
100 yards / 200 yards	Dry Fire X 10: Y / N	Time:	**Score:**	**# of X's:**	

Date:	Rifle:	Scope:	Elev:	Wind:	Notes:
100 yards / 200 yards	Dry Fire X 10: Y / N	Time:	**Score:**	**# of X's:**	

N.P.A. Drill - 4

Precision Rifle ©

SPEED DOTS

Purpose: To quickly establish a solid prone position, good NPA and proper follow through.

Distance: 100 Yards.

Target: KYRL (only one row is needed)

Extra Equipment Needed: Shot timer.

Rounds Fired Per Stage: 2 Rounds.   **Total Rounds Fired:** 10 Rounds.

Point Penalty: Go / No Go (2 Rounds must be in or touching the circle to pass.)

Repetitions: 1 Rep of 5 stages.

Starting Position & Condition: Standing 10 feet behind your rifle. Condition 1.

Description: Place rifle and equipment on the firing line. At the timer beep, assume a good shooting position and engage the largest circle with 2 rounds in a par time of **7 seconds.** Put rifle on safe and stand. At the timer beep, assume a good shooting position and engage the 2nd largest circle with 2 rounds in a par time of **10 seconds.** Put rifle on safe and stand. At the timer beep, assume a good shooting position and engage the 3rd largest circle with 2 rounds in a par time of **14 seconds.** Put rifle on safe and stand. At the timer beep, assume a good shooting position and engage the 4th largest circle with 2 rounds in a par time of **18 seconds.** Put rifle on safe and stand. At the timer beep, assume a good shooting position and engage the smallest circle with 2 rounds in a par time of **22 seconds.** Put rifle on safe and stand.

Goals: Novice: Top 3 dots under par.   Expert: Top 4 dots under par.   Gunfighter: All dots under par.

Variation: Try support side.

SPEED DOTS

Date:	Location:	Rifle:	Scope:	Mag Power X:
Ammo:	Support Type:		Dominant Side / Support Side	
(Dot 1) 7 Sec Par: Y / N	(Dot 2) 10 Sec Par: Y / N	(Dot 3) 14 Sec Par: Y / N	(Dot 4) 18 Sec Par: Y / N	(Dot 5) 22 Sec Par: Y / N
(Dot 1) 2 rounds in: Y / N	(Dot 2) 2 rounds in: Y / N	(Dot 3) 2 rounds in: Y / N	(Dot 4) 2 rounds in: Y / N	(Dot 5) 2 rounds in: Y / N
Notes:				**Best Dot Under Par:**

Date:	Location:	Rifle:	Scope:	Mag Power X:
Ammo:	Support Type:		Dominant Side / Support Side	
(Dot 1) 7 Sec Par: Y / N	(Dot 2) 10 Sec Par: Y / N	(Dot 3) 14 Sec Par: Y / N	(Dot 4) 18 Sec Par: Y / N	(Dot 5) 22 Sec Par: Y / N
(Dot 1) 2 rounds in: Y / N	(Dot 2) 2 rounds in: Y / N	(Dot 3) 2 rounds in: Y / N	(Dot 4) 2 rounds in: Y / N	(Dot 5) 2 rounds in: Y / N
Notes:				**Best Dot Under Par:**

Date:	Location:	Rifle:	Scope:	Mag Power X:
Ammo:	Support Type:		Dominant Side / Support Side	
(Dot 1) 7 Sec Par: Y / N	(Dot 2) 10 Sec Par: Y / N	(Dot 3) 14 Sec Par: Y / N	(Dot 4) 18 Sec Par: Y / N	(Dot 5) 22 Sec Par: Y / N
(Dot 1) 2 rounds in: Y / N	(Dot 2) 2 rounds in: Y / N	(Dot 3) 2 rounds in: Y / N	(Dot 4) 2 rounds in: Y / N	(Dot 5) 2 rounds in: Y / N
Notes:				**Best Dot Under Par:**

SPEED DOTS

www.GUNFIGHTERSERIES.com ©

Date:	Location:	Rifle:	Scope:	Mag Power X:
Ammo:	Support Type:		Dominant Side / Support Side	
(Dot 1) 7 Sec Par: Y / N	(Dot 2) 10 Sec Par: Y / N	(Dot 3) 14 Sec Par: Y / N	(Dot 4) 18 Sec Par: Y / N	(Dot 5) 22 Sec Par: Y / N
(Dot 1) 2 rounds in: Y / N	(Dot 2) 2 rounds in: Y / N	(Dot 3) 2 rounds in: Y / N	(Dot 4) 2 rounds in: Y / N	(Dot 5) 2 rounds in: Y / N
Notes:				**Best Dot Under Par:**

Date:	Location:	Rifle:	Scope:	Mag Power X:
Ammo:	Support Type:		Dominant Side / Support Side	
(Dot 1) 7 Sec Par: Y / N	(Dot 2) 10 Sec Par: Y / N	(Dot 3) 14 Sec Par: Y / N	(Dot 4) 18 Sec Par: Y / N	(Dot 5) 22 Sec Par: Y / N
(Dot 1) 2 rounds in: Y / N	(Dot 2) 2 rounds in: Y / N	(Dot 3) 2 rounds in: Y / N	(Dot 4) 2 rounds in: Y / N	(Dot 5) 2 rounds in: Y / N
Notes:				**Best Dot Under Par:**

Date:	Location:	Rifle:	Scope:	Mag Power X:
Ammo:	Support Type:		Dominant Side / Support Side	
(Dot 1) 7 Sec Par: Y / N	(Dot 2) 10 Sec Par: Y / N	(Dot 3) 14 Sec Par: Y / N	(Dot 4) 18 Sec Par: Y / N	(Dot 5) 22 Sec Par: Y / N
(Dot 1) 2 rounds in: Y / N	(Dot 2) 2 rounds in: Y / N	(Dot 3) 2 rounds in: Y / N	(Dot 4) 2 rounds in: Y / N	(Dot 5) 2 rounds in: Y / N
Notes:				**Best Dot Under Par:**

SPEED DOTS

Date:	Location:	Rifle:	Scope:	Mag Power X:
Ammo:	Support Type:		Dominant Side / Support Side	
(Dot 1) 7 Sec Par: Y / N	(Dot 2) 10 Sec Par: Y / N	(Dot 3) 14 Sec Par: Y / N	(Dot 4) 18 Sec Par: Y / N	(Dot 5) 22 Sec Par: Y / N
(Dot 1) 2 rounds in: Y / N	(Dot 2) 2 rounds in: Y / N	(Dot 3) 2 rounds in: Y / N	(Dot 4) 2 rounds in: Y / N	(Dot 5) 2 rounds in: Y / N
Notes:				**Best Dot Under Par:**

Date:	Location:	Rifle:	Scope:	Mag Power X:
Ammo:	Support Type:		Dominant Side / Support Side	
(Dot 1) 7 Sec Par: Y / N	(Dot 2) 10 Sec Par: Y / N	(Dot 3) 14 Sec Par: Y / N	(Dot 4) 18 Sec Par: Y / N	(Dot 5) 22 Sec Par: Y / N
(Dot 1) 2 rounds in: Y / N	(Dot 2) 2 rounds in: Y / N	(Dot 3) 2 rounds in: Y / N	(Dot 4) 2 rounds in: Y / N	(Dot 5) 2 rounds in: Y / N
Notes:				**Best Dot Under Par:**

Date:	Location:	Rifle:	Scope:	Mag Power X:
Ammo:	Support Type:		Dominant Side / Support Side	
(Dot 1) 7 Sec Par: Y / N	(Dot 2) 10 Sec Par: Y / N	(Dot 3) 14 Sec Par: Y / N	(Dot 4) 18 Sec Par: Y / N	(Dot 5) 22 Sec Par: Y / N
(Dot 1) 2 rounds in: Y / N	(Dot 2) 2 rounds in: Y / N	(Dot 3) 2 rounds in: Y / N	(Dot 4) 2 rounds in: Y / N	(Dot 5) 2 rounds in: Y / N
Notes:				**Best Dot Under Par:**

N.P.A. Drill - 5

Precision Rifle ©

SPEED DOTS

Date:	Location:	Rifle:	Scope:	Mag Power X:
Ammo:	Support Type:		Dominant Side / Support Side	
(Dot 1) 7 Sec Par: Y / N	(Dot 2) 10 Sec Par: Y / N	(Dot 3) 14 Sec Par: Y / N	(Dot 4) 18 Sec Par: Y / N	(Dot 5) 22 Sec Par: Y / N
(Dot 1) 2 rounds in: Y / N	(Dot 2) 2 rounds in: Y / N	(Dot 3) 2 rounds in: Y / N	(Dot 4) 2 rounds in: Y / N	(Dot 5) 2 rounds in: Y / N
Notes:				**Best Dot Under Par:**

Date:	Location:	Rifle:	Scope:	Mag Power X:
Ammo:	Support Type:		Dominant Side / Support Side	
(Dot 1) 7 Sec Par: Y / N	(Dot 2) 10 Sec Par: Y / N	(Dot 3) 14 Sec Par: Y / N	(Dot 4) 18 Sec Par: Y / N	(Dot 5) 22 Sec Par: Y / N
(Dot 1) 2 rounds in: Y / N	(Dot 2) 2 rounds in: Y / N	(Dot 3) 2 rounds in: Y / N	(Dot 4) 2 rounds in: Y / N	(Dot 5) 2 rounds in: Y / N
Notes:				**Best Dot Under Par:**

Date:	Location:	Rifle:	Scope:	Mag Power X:
Ammo:	Support Type:		Dominant Side / Support Side	
(Dot 1) 7 Sec Par: Y / N	(Dot 2) 10 Sec Par: Y / N	(Dot 3) 14 Sec Par: Y / N	(Dot 4) 18 Sec Par: Y / N	(Dot 5) 22 Sec Par: Y / N
(Dot 1) 2 rounds in: Y / N	(Dot 2) 2 rounds in: Y / N	(Dot 3) 2 rounds in: Y / N	(Dot 4) 2 rounds in: Y / N	(Dot 5) 2 rounds in: Y / N
Notes:				**Best Dot Under Par:**

SPEED DOTS

Date:	Location:	Rifle:	Scope:	Mag Power X:
Ammo:	Support Type:		Dominant Side / Support Side	
(Dot 1) 7 Sec Par: Y / N	(Dot 2) 10 Sec Par: Y / N	(Dot 3) 14 Sec Par: Y / N	(Dot 4) 18 Sec Par: Y / N	(Dot 5) 22 Sec Par: Y / N
(Dot 1) 2 rounds in: Y / N	(Dot 2) 2 rounds in: Y / N	(Dot 3) 2 rounds in: Y / N	(Dot 4) 2 rounds in: Y / N	(Dot 5) 2 rounds in: Y / N
Notes:				**Best Dot Under Par:**

Date:	Location:	Rifle:	Scope:	Mag Power X:
Ammo:	Support Type:		Dominant Side / Support Side	
(Dot 1) 7 Sec Par: Y / N	(Dot 2) 10 Sec Par: Y / N	(Dot 3) 14 Sec Par: Y / N	(Dot 4) 18 Sec Par: Y / N	(Dot 5) 22 Sec Par: Y / N
(Dot 1) 2 rounds in: Y / N	(Dot 2) 2 rounds in: Y / N	(Dot 3) 2 rounds in: Y / N	(Dot 4) 2 rounds in: Y / N	(Dot 5) 2 rounds in: Y / N
Notes:				**Best Dot Under Par:**

Date:	Location:	Rifle:	Scope:	Mag Power X:
Ammo:	Support Type:		Dominant Side / Support Side	
(Dot 1) 7 Sec Par: Y / N	(Dot 2) 10 Sec Pa: Y / N	(Dot 3) 14 Sec Par: Y / N	(Dot 4) 18 Sec Par: Y / N	(Dot 5) 22 Sec Par: Y / N
(Dot 1) 2 rounds in: Y / N	(Dot 2) 2 rounds in: Y / N	(Dot 3) 2 rounds in: Y / N	(Dot 4) 2 rounds in: Y / N	(Dot 5) 2 rounds in: Y / N
Notes:				**Best Dot Under Par:**

Precision Rifle ©

SCOPE TURRET DRILLS

Purpose: To master your equipment's mechanics.

Extra Equipment Needed: Shot timer and shooting partner to read the drill.

Total Rounds Fired: 0 Rounds.

Repetitions: 5 Reps.

Starting Position & Condition: Prone position. Condition 4.

Description: Start each rep with scope turrets on ZERO. Maintain full sight picture and proper eye relief while never breaking cheek weld during the entire drill. Make the scope turret adjustments as commanded by the spotter, while confirming the adjustment out loud. EXAMPLE: "3 UP and 2 LEFT." Maintain sight picture, squeeze trigger, cycle the bolt and then make the next scope adjustments as commanded. Continue until the rep is complete. Upon dry firing after last adjustment your scope turret should be on the prescribed end reading, if not you fail. If no spotter is available to assist, place the drill page next to your rifle to easily read the drill without looking at your turrets.

Variations: Try doing the drill with your eyes closed while making your scope adjustments.

Disclaimer: Typically you want to communicate elevation and windage adjustments in a unit of measure (MIL or MOA). For this drill simply use number of clicks.

Goals: Novice: Perfect reps under 100 seconds. Expert: Perfect reps under 60 seconds. Gunfighter: Perfect reps under 45 seconds.

Rep 1	Rep 2	Rep 3	Rep 4	Rep 5
3U 2L	6U 4R	2U 2R	5U 3L	12U 8L
6U 6R	10U 8L	3U 3L	2D 6R	20U 16R
5D 2L	5D 6L	2D 2L	8U 2R	10D 12R
2U 4R	3U 8R	1D 4R	3D 4L	6U 16L
6D 6L	9D 3L	2D 1L	6D 3L	18D 6R
0 / 0 END	5U 5L END	0/0 END	2U 2L END	10U 10R END

SCOPE TURRET DRILLS

Date:	Weapon:	Scope:	Eyes Open: Y / N	Notes:
Rep 1: Go / No Go	Rep 2: Go / No Go	Rep 3: Go / No Go	Rep 4: Go / No Go	Rep 5: Go / No Go
Date:	Weapon:	Scope:	Eyes Open: Y / N	Notes:
Rep 1: Go / No Go	Rep 2: Go / No Go	Rep 3: Go / No Go	Rep 4: Go / No Go	Rep 5: Go / No Go
Date:	Weapon:	Scope:	Eyes Open: Y / N	Notes:
Rep 1: Go / No Go	Rep 2: Go / No Go	Rep 3: Go / No Go	Rep 4: Go / No Go	Rep 5: Go / No Go
Date:	Weapon:	Scope:	Eyes Open: Y / N	Notes:
Rep 1: Go / No Go	Rep 2: Go / No Go	Rep 3: Go / No Go	Rep 4: Go / No Go	Rep 5: Go / No Go
Date:	Weapon:	Scope:	Eyes Open: Y / N	Notes:
Rep 1: Go / No Go	Rep 2: Go / No Go	Rep 3: Go / No Go	Rep 4: Go / No Go	Rep 5: Go / No Go
Date:	Weapon:	Scope:	Eyes Open: Y / N	Notes:
Rep 1: Go / No Go	Rep 2: Go / No Go	Rep 3: Go / No Go	Rep 4: Go / No Go	Rep 5: Go / No Go

Precision Rifle ©

Scope Drill - 1

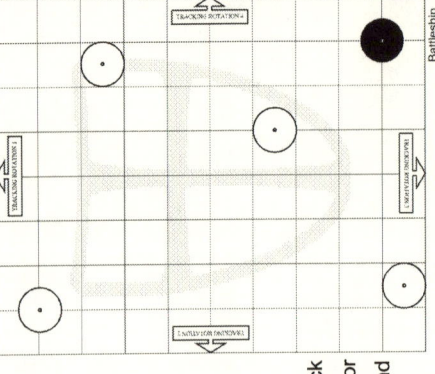

BATTLESHIP

Purpose: Improve ability to quickly measure and adjust for corrections and secondary targets.

Distance: 100 Yards.

Target: Battleship

Starting Position & Condition: Standing behind your rifle. Condition 1.

Description: On your own personal go assume a good prone position with scope on 100 yard zero and fire 1 round into the black dot. Count the distance up/down and left/right to the next circle in a clockwise pattern. Make a scope turret adjustments to correct for the next target. Keeping your aiming point on the original black dot, fire 1 round. Impact should be in the white circle which you had just adjusted for. If not, make another correction based off of your missed impact.

Continue on by measuring distance from the last impact to the next white circle in a clockwise patter. Aiming at the original black dot the entire time. Finish the exercise by returning back to the black dot to fire 1 last round. Your scope should be back on your 100 yard zero.

Goals: Novice: Completed in 10 rounds or under.   Expert: Completed with no misses.   Gunfighter: Completed with no misses without looking at turrets.

Variations:

⊕ Rotate the target 90° each time for variation. Scopes with ZERO stops can only use target rotation 1 & 2.

⊕ Adjust distance to target.

⊕ Time yourself for personal best with no misses.

BATTLESHIP

Date:	Location:	Rifle:	Scope:	Notes
Target Distance:	Target Rotation #:	Time:	Number of Misses:	
Date:	Location:	Rifle:	Scope:	Notes
Target Distance:	Target Rotation #:	Time:	Number of Misses:	
Date:	Location:	Rifle:	Scope:	Notes
Target Distance:	Target Rotation #:	Time:	Number of Misses:	
Date:	Location:	Rifle:	Scope:	Notes
Target Distance:	Target Rotation #:	Time:	Number of Misses:	
Date:	Location:	Rifle:	Scope:	Notes
Target Distance:	Target Rotation #:	Time:	Number of Misses:	
Date:	Location:	Rifle:	Scope:	Notes
Target Distance:	Target Rotation #:	Time:	Number of Misses:	
Date:	Location:	Rifle:	Scope:	Notes
Target Distance:	Target Rotation #:	Time:	Number of Misses:	
Date:	Location:	Rifle:	Scope:	Notes
Target Distance:	Target Rotation #:	Time:	Number of Misses:	
Date:	Location:	Rifle:	Scope:	Notes
Target Distance:	Target Rotation #:	Time:	Number of Misses:	
Date:	Location:	Rifle:	Scope:	Notes
Target Distance:	Target Rotation #:	Time:	Number of Misses:	

Precision Rifle ©

Scope Drill - 2

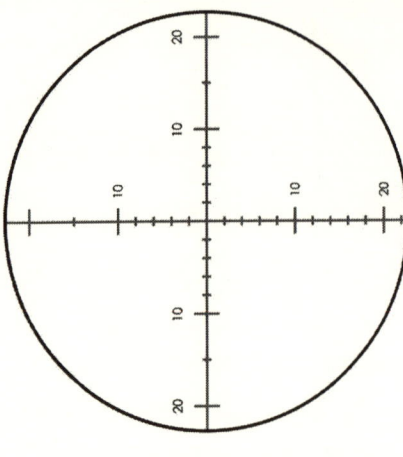

COME UP QUICK

Purpose: Mastering your ballistics chart and reticle familiarization.

Total Rounds Fired: 0 Rounds.

Point Penalty: Go / No Go.

Starting Position & Condition: Any. Condition 4.

Description: Given a list of targets distances, without aid or reference, for each target write down your elevation come up and windage adjustment for a full value 10 MPH wind as well as plot your hold overs and wind holds on the provided MOA or MIL reticle diagram. After completed with this test, check your answers using your ballistics chart or ballistics calculator for current weather conditions. A wrong answer equals a waisted round down range so the goal is to be accurate within margin of error.

Goals: Novice: Within 1 MOA or 0.3 Mil. Expert: Within 1/2 MOA or 0.2 Mil. Gunfighter: Within 1/4 MOA or 0.1 Mil.

Variations: You may swap out the provided reticle diagram with your own factory reticle diagram for better training tailored to you.

www.GUNFIGHTERSERIES.com ©

COME UP QUICK

Rifle: **Ammo:**   **Date:**   **Unit of Measurement:** MOA / MIL

Temp: **Baro:**   **MV:**

Target	Yards / Meters	Elevation Guess	True Elevation	10 MPH Guess	True Windage
1	135				
2	225				
3	290				
4	345				
5	410				
6	475				
7	515				
8	590				
9	660				
10	710				
11	770				
12	825				
13	865				
14	910				
15	985				
	Number Correct:		**Number Correct:**		

Scope Drill - 3

Precision Rifle ©

www.GUNFIGHTERSERIES.com ©

COME UP QUICK

Rifle: _____ Ammo: _____ Date: _____ Unit of Measurement: MOA / MIL Temp: _____ Baro: _____ MV: _____

Target	Yards / Meters	Elevation Guess	True Elevation	10 MPH Guess	True Windage
1	185				
2	250				
3	310				
4	360				
5	440				
6	495				
7	535				
8	580				
9	635				
10	690				
11	720				
12	785				
13	840				
14	960				
15	1050				
		Number Correct:		**Number Correct:**	

EBR-1 MOA

EBR-1 MRAD

COME UP QUICK

Rifle: _____ Ammo: _____ Date: _____ Unit of Measurement: MOA / MIL

Temp: _____ Baro: _____ MV: _____

Target	Yards / Meters	Elevation Guess	True Elevation	10 MPH Guess	True Windage
1	65				
2	155				
3	240				
4	320				
5	455				
6	475				
7	560				
8	625				
9	670				
10	735				
11	790				
12	845				
13	880				
14	935				
15	1035				

Number Correct: _____ Number Correct: _____

Scope Drill - 3

Precision Rifle ©

COME UP QUICK

www.GUNFIGHTERSERIES.com ©

Rifle:	Ammo:	Date:	Unit of Measurement: MOA / MIL			
		Temp:	Baro:	MV:		
Target	Yards / Meters	Elevation Guess	True Elevation	10 MPH Guess	True Windage	
1	55					
2	135					
3	260					
4	325					
5	385					
6	440					
7	505					
8	565					
9	615					
10	690					
11	750					
12	820					
13	860					
14	910					
15	950					
		Number Correct:		Number Correct:		

EBR-1 MOA

EBR-1 MRAD

COME UP QUICK

Rifle: _____ Ammo: _____ Date: _____ Unit of Measurement: MOA / MIL

Temp: _____ Baro: _____ MV: _____

Target	Yards / Meters	Elevation Guess	True Elevation	10 MPH Guess	True Windage
1	210				
2	370				
3	555				
4	625				
5	680				
6	725				
7	770				
8	835				
9	850				
10	880				
11	925				
12	960				
13	990				
14	1025				
15	1100				

Number Correct: _____   Number Correct: _____

Scope Drill - 3

Precision Rifle ©

COLD BORE + 4

By: Bob Corby, Marksmanship Training Center

Purpose: Determine and record cold bore offset and measure group size.

Distance: 100 Yards.

Target: 3/4 inch dots X 2.

Total Rounds Fired: 5 Rounds.

Repetitions: 2 Reps.

Starting Position & Condition: Prone. Condition 1.

Description: Record atmospherics and turret settings if on ZERO or adjusted for CB (Cold Bore) / CCB (Clean Cold Bore). Fire 1 round into a 3/4 inch circle target. Without making any scope adjustments immediately fire 4 more rounds into the second 3/4 inch circle target. Record group size. Record the CB or CCB offset difference up / down and left / right from the center of the 4 round group.

Note: If your zero shifts each training day; retorque rifle and scope ring screws, focus on a good NPA and check for parallax.

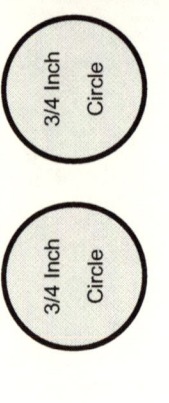

COLD BORE + 4

Date:	Rifle	Scope:	Ammo:
Temp:	Baro:	Alt Density:	CB / CCB
Elev: Wind:	Group Size:	CB Difference: U / D	L / R
Date:	Rifle	Scope:	Ammo:
Temp:	Baro:	Alt Density:	CB / CCB
Elev: Wind:	Group Size:	CB Difference: U / D	L / R
Date:	Rifle	Scope:	Ammo:
Temp:	Baro:	Alt Density:	CB / CCB
Elev: Wind:	Group Size:	CB Difference: U / D	L / R
Date:	Rifle	Scope:	Ammo:
Temp:	Baro:	Alt Density:	CB / CCB
Elev: Wind:	Group Size:	CB Difference: U / D	L / R
Date:	Rifle	Scope:	Ammo:
Temp:	Baro:	Alt Density:	CB / CCB
Elev: Wind:	Group Size:	CB Difference: U / D	L / R

Accuracy Drill - 1

Precision Rifle ©

COLD BORE + 4

Date:	Rifle	Scope:	Ammo:	
Temp:	Baro:	Alt Density:		CB / CCB
Elev: Wind:	Group Size:	CB Difference:	U / D	L / R
Date:	Rifle	Scope:	Ammo:	
Temp:	Baro:	Alt Density:		CB / CCB
Elev: Wind:	Group Size:	CB Difference:	U / D	L / R
Date:	Rifle	Scope:	Ammo:	
Temp:	Baro:	Alt Density:		CB / CCB
Elev: Wind:	Group Size:	CB Difference:	U / D	L / R
Date:	Rifle	Scope:	Ammo:	
Temp:	Baro:	Alt Density:		CB / CCB
Elev: Wind:	Group Size:	CB Difference:	U / D	L / R
Date:	Rifle	Scope:	Ammo:	
Temp:	Baro:	Alt Density:		CB / CCB
Elev: Wind:	Group Size:	CB Difference:	U / D	L / R

www.GUNFIGHTERSERIES.com ©

COLD BORE + 4

Date:	Rifle:	Scope:	Ammo:
Temp:	Baro:	Alt Density:	CB / CCB
Elev: Wind:	Group Size:	CB Difference: U / D	L / R
Date:	Rifle:	Scope:	Ammo:
Temp:	Baro:	Alt Density:	CB / CCB
Elev: Wind:	Group Size:	CB Difference: U / D	L / R
Date:	Rifle:	Scope:	Ammo:
Temp:	Baro:	Alt Density:	CB / CCB
Elev: Wind:	Group Size:	CB Difference: U / D	L / R
Date:	Rifle:	Scope:	Ammo:
Temp:	Baro:	Alt Density:	CB / CCB
Elev: Wind:	Group Size:	CB Difference: U / D	L / R
Date:	Rifle:	Scope:	Ammo:
Temp:	Baro:	Alt Density:	CB / CCB
Elev: Wind:	Group Size:	CB Difference: U / D	L / R

Accuracy Drill - 1

Precision Rifle ©

COLD BORE + 4

Date:	Rifle	Scope:		Ammo:	
Temp:	Baro:	Alt Density:	U / D	CB / CCB	L / R
Elev:	Wind:	Group Size:	CB Difference:		
Date:	Rifle	Scope:		Ammo:	
Temp:	Baro:	Alt Density:	U / D	CB / CCB	L / R
Elev:	Wind:	Group Size:	CB Difference:		
Date:	Rifle	Scope:		Ammo:	
Temp:	Baro:	Alt Density:	U / D	CB / CCB	L / R
Elev:	Wind:	Group Size:	CB Difference:		
Date:	Rifle	Scope:		Ammo:	
Temp:	Baro:	Alt Density:	U / D	CB / CCB	L / R
Elev:	Wind:	Group Size:	CB Difference:		
Date:	Rifle	Scope:		Ammo:	
Temp:	Baro:	Alt Density:	U / D	CB / CCB	L / R
Elev:	Wind:	Group Size:	CB Difference:		

COLD BORE + 4

Date:	Rifle	Scope:	Ammo:	
Temp:	Baro:	Alt Density:		CB / CCB
Elev: Wind:	Group Size:	CB Difference:	U / D	L / R
Date:	Rifle	Scope:	Ammo:	
Temp:	Baro:	Alt Density:		CB / CCB
Elev: Wind:	Group Size:	CB Difference:	U / D	L / R
Date:	Rifle	Scope:	Ammo:	
Temp:	Baro:	Alt Density:		CB / CCB
Elev: Wind:	Group Size:	CB Difference:	U / D	L / R
Date:	Rifle	Scope:	Ammo:	
Temp:	Baro:	Alt Density:		CB / CCB
Elev: Wind:	Group Size:	CB Difference:	U / D	L / R
Date:	Rifle	Scope:	Ammo:	
Temp:	Baro:	Alt Density:		CB / CCB
Elev: Wind:	Group Size:	CB Difference:	U / D	L / R

Accuracy Drill - 1

PRECISION GINGY NINJI

By: Danny Rilett, Marksmanship Training Center

Purpose: To reinforce and enhance all marksmanship fundamentals. Excellent warm up drill.

Distance: 100 Yards.

Target: 1 Inch dots X 4

Total Rounds Fired: 10 Rounds.

Point Penalty: Go / No Go.

Repetitions: 4 Reps.

Starting Position & Condition: Prone. Condition 1.

Description: Assume a good prone position. Dry fire 4 times, then fire 1 round into the 1st dot. Dry fire 3 times, then fire 2 rounds into the 2nd dot. Dry fire 2 times, then fire 3 rounds into the 3rd dot. Dry fire 1 time, fire 4 rounds into the 4th dot.

Goals: All shots in the dots with tight shot groups.

Variations: Add a 5th dot, starting with dry firing 5 times with 1 live shot.

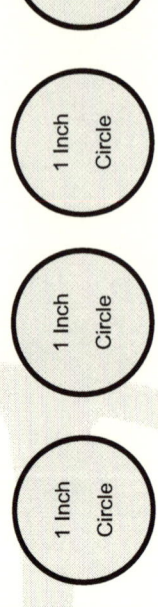

www.GUNFIGHTERSERIES.com ©

PRECISION GINGY NINJI

Date:	Rifle:	Scope:	Ammo:	Elev:	Wind:
Dot 1: Go / No Go	Dot 2: Go / No Go	Dot 3: Go / No Go	Dot 4: Go / No Go	Notes:	

Date:	Rifle:	Scope:	Ammo:	Elev:	Wind:
Dot 1: Go / No Go	Dot 2: Go / No Go	Dot 3: Go / No Go	Dot 4: Go / No Go	Notes:	

Date:	Rifle:	Scope:	Ammo:	Elev:	Wind:
Dot 1: Go / No Go	Dot 2: Go / No Go	Dot 3: Go / No Go	Dot 4: Go / No Go	Notes:	

Date:	Rifle:	Scope:	Ammo:	Elev:	Wind:
Dot 1: Go / No Go	Dot 2: Go / No Go	Dot 3: Go / No Go	Dot 4: Go / No Go	Notes:	

Date:	Rifle:	Scope:	Ammo:	Elev:	Wind:
Dot 1: Go / No Go	Dot 2: Go / No Go	Dot 3: Go / No Go	Dot 4: Go / No Go	Notes:	

Date:	Rifle:	Scope:	Ammo:	Elev:	Wind:
Dot 1: Go / No Go	Dot 2: Go / No Go	Dot 3: Go / No Go	Dot 4: Go / No Go	Notes:	

Precision Rifle ©

Accuracy Drill - 2

PRECISION GINGY NINJI

www.GUNFIGHTERSERIES.com ©

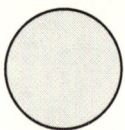

Date:	Rifle:	Scope:	Ammo:	Elev:	Wind:
Dot 1: Go / No Go	Dot 2: Go / No Go	Dot 3: Go / No Go	Dot 4: Go / No Go	Notes:	

Date:	Rifle:	Scope:	Ammo:	Elev:	Wind:
Dot 1: Go / No Go	Dot 2: Go / No Go	Dot 3: Go / No Go	Dot 4: Go / No Go	Notes:	

Date:	Rifle:	Scope:	Ammo:	Elev:	Wind:
Dot 1: Go / No Go	Dot 2: Go / No Go	Dot 3: Go / No Go	Dot 4: Go / No Go	Notes:	

Date:	Rifle:	Scope:	Ammo:	Elev:	Wind:
Dot 1: Go / No Go	Dot 2: Go / No Go	Dot 3: Go / No Go	Dot 4: Go / No Go	Notes:	

Date:	Rifle:	Scope:	Ammo:	Elev:	Wind:
Dot 1: Go / No Go	Dot 2: Go / No Go	Dot 3: Go / No Go	Dot 4: Go / No Go	Notes:	

Date:	Rifle:	Scope:	Ammo:	Elev:	Wind:
Dot 1: Go / No Go	Dot 2: Go / No Go	Dot 3: Go / No Go	Dot 4: Go / No Go	Notes:	

PRECISION GINGY NINJI

Date:	Rifle:	Scope:	Ammo:	Elev:	Wind:
Dot 1: Go / No Go	Dot 2: Go / No Go	Dot 3: Go / No Go	Dot 4: Go / No Go	Notes:	

Date:	Rifle:	Scope:	Ammo:	Elev:	Wind:
Dot 1: Go / No Go	Dot 2: Go / No Go	Dot 3: Go / No Go	Dot 4: Go / No Go	Notes:	

Date:	Rifle:	Scope:	Ammo:	Elev:	Wind:
Dot 1: Go / No Go	Dot 2: Go / No Go	Dot 3: Go / No Go	Dot 4: Go / No Go	Notes:	

Date:	Rifle:	Scope:	Ammo:	Elev:	Wind:
Dot 1: Go / No Go	Dot 2: Go / No Go	Dot 3: Go / No Go	Dot 4: Go / No Go	Notes:	

Date:	Rifle:	Scope:	Ammo:	Elev:	Wind:
Dot 1: Go / No Go	Dot 2: Go / No Go	Dot 3: Go / No Go	Dot 4: Go / No Go	Notes:	

Date:	Rifle:	Scope:	Ammo:	Elev:	Wind:
Dot 1: Go / No Go	Dot 2: Go / No Go	Dot 3: Go / No Go	Dot 4: Go / No Go	Notes:	

Accuracy Drill - 2

Precision Rifle ©

PRECISION GINGY NINJI

Date:	Rifle:	Scope:	Ammo:	Elev:	Wind:
Dot 1: Go / No Go	Dot 2: Go / No Go	Dot 3: Go / No Go	Dot 4: Go / No Go	Notes:	

Date:	Rifle:	Scope:	Ammo:	Elev:	Wind:
Dot 1: Go / No Go	Dot 2: Go / No Go	Dot 3: Go / No Go	Dot 4: Go / No Go	Notes:	

Date:	Rifle:	Scope:	Ammo:	Elev:	Wind:
Dot 1: Go / No Go	Dot 2: Go / No Go	Dot 3: Go / No Go	Dot 4: Go / No Go	Notes:	

Date:	Rifle:	Scope:	Ammo:	Elev:	Wind:
Dot 1: Go / No Go	Dot 2: Go / No Go	Dot 3: Go / No Go	Dot 4: Go / No Go	Notes:	

Date:	Rifle:	Scope:	Ammo:	Elev:	Wind:
Dot 1: Go / No Go	Dot 2: Go / No Go	Dot 3: Go / No Go	Dot 4: Go / No Go	Notes:	

Date:	Rifle:	Scope:	Ammo:	Elev:	Wind:
Dot 1: Go / No Go	Dot 2: Go / No Go	Dot 3: Go / No Go	Dot 4: Go / No Go	Notes:	

www.GUNFIGHTERSERIES.com ©

PRECISION GINGY NINJI

Date:	Rifle:	Scope:	Ammo:	Elev:	Wind:
Dot 1: Go / No Go	Dot 2: Go / No Go	Dot 3: Go / No Go	Dot 4: Go / No Go	Notes:	

Date:	Rifle:	Scope:	Ammo:	Elev:	Wind:
Dot 1: Go / No Go	Dot 2: Go / No Go	Dot 3: Go / No Go	Dot 4: Go / No Go	Notes:	

Date:	Rifle:	Scope:	Ammo:	Elev:	Wind:
Dot 1: Go / No Go	Dot 2: Go / No Go	Dot 3: Go / No Go	Dot 4: Go / No Go	Notes:	

Date:	Rifle:	Scope:	Ammo:	Elev:	Wind:
Dot 1: Go / No Go	Dot 2: Go / No Go	Dot 3: Go / No Go	Dot 4: Go / No Go	Notes:	

Date:	Rifle:	Scope:	Ammo:	Elev:	Wind:
Dot 1: Go / No Go	Dot 2: Go / No Go	Dot 3: Go / No Go	Dot 4: Go / No Go	Notes:	

Date:	Rifle:	Scope:	Ammo:	Elev:	Wind:
Dot 1: Go / No Go	Dot 2: Go / No Go	Dot 3: Go / No Go	Dot 4: Go / No Go	Notes:	

Accuracy Drill - 2

Precision Rifle ©

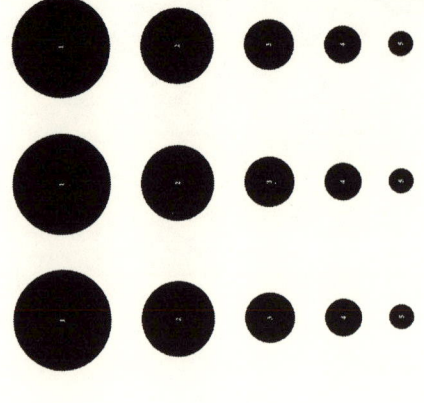

KNOW YOUR PRONE LIMIT

Purpose: To learn and test your prone repeatable accuracy limit.

Distance: 100 Yards.

Target: KYRL

Rounds Fired Per Stage: 1 to 5 Rounds.

Total Rounds Fired: 3 to 15 Rounds.

Point Penalty: As per target score. Score is zeroed out for any miss off black.

Repetitions: 1 Rep of 3 stages.

Starting Position & Condition: Prone. Condition 1.

Description: On your own personal go from a good prone shooting position, either supported or with a sling, fire 1 practice round into each dot on the far left column starting from the biggest on top to the smallest on bottom. Log your accuracy dot size limit.

On your own personal go fire 1 round into each dot in the middle column starting at the biggest on top to the smallest dot you feel certain to hit. Log your accuracy dot size limit. Score is automatically zeroed out for any miss off black.

On your own personal go fire 1 round into each dot in the far right column starting at the biggest on top to the smallest dot you feel certain to hit. Log your accuracy dot size limit. Score is automatically zeroed out for any miss off black.

Goals: Improve your personal best with all types of support.

www.gunfighterseries.com ©

KNOW YOUR PRONE LIMITS

Date:		Location:		Rifle:	Scope:	Ammo:
Rep 1 Best Dot:	2" / 1.5" / 1" / .75" / .5"				Supported / Sling	Support Type:
Rep 2 Best Dot:	2" / 1.5" / 1" / .75" / .5"			Rep 2 Score:		Total # of rounds out:
Rep 3 Best Dot:	2" / 1.5" / 1" / .75" / .5"			Rep 3 Score:		**Total Score:**
Notes:						

Date:		Location:		Rifle:	Scope:	Ammo:
Rep 1 Best Dot:	2" / 1.5" / 1" / .75" / .5"				Supported / Sling	Support Type:
Rep 2 Best Dot:	2" / 1.5" / 1" / .75" / .5"			Rep 2 Score:		Total # of rounds out:
Rep 3 Best Dot:	2" / 1.5" / 1" / .75" / .5"			Rep 3 Score:		**Total Score:**
Notes:						

Date:		Location:		Rifle:	Scope:	Ammo:
Rep 1 Best Dot:	2" / 1.5" / 1" / .75" / .5"				Supported / Sling	Support Type:
Rep 2 Best Dot:	2" / 1.5" / 1" / .75" / .5"			Rep 2 Score:		Total # of rounds out:
Rep 3 Best Dot:	2" / 1.5" / 1" / .75" / .5"			Rep 3 Score:		**Total Score:**
Notes:						

Precision Rifle ©

Accuracy Drill - 3

KNOW YOUR PRONE LIMITS

Date:	Location:	Rifle:	Scope:	Ammo:
Rep 1 Best Dot:	2" / 1.5" / 1" / .75" / .5"		Supported / Sling	Support Type:
Rep 2 Best Dot:	2" / 1.5" / 1" / .75" / .5"	Rep 2 Score:		Total # of rounds out:
Rep 3 Best Dot:	2" / 1.5" / 1" / .75" / .5"	Rep 3 Score:		**Total Score:**
Notes:				

Date:	Location:	Rifle:	Scope:	Ammo:
Rep 1 Best Dot:	2" / 1.5" / 1" / .75" / .5"		Supported / Sling	Support Type:
Rep 2 Best Dot:	2" / 1.5" / 1" / .75" / .5"	Rep 2 Score:		Total # of rounds out:
Rep 3 Best Dot:	2" / 1.5" / 1" / .75" / .5"	Rep 3 Score:		**Total Score:**
Notes:				

Date:	Location:	Rifle:	Scope:	Ammo:
Rep 1 Best Dot:	2" / 1.5" / 1" / .75" / .5"		Supported / Sling	Support Type:
Rep 2 Best Dot:	2" / 1.5" / 1" / .75" / .5"	Rep 2 Score:		Total # of rounds out:
Rep 3 Best Dot:	2" / 1.5" / 1" / .75" / .5"	Rep 3 Score:		**Total Score:**
Notes:				

www.GUNFIGHTERSERIES.com ©

KNOW YOUR PRONE LIMITS

Date:	Location:	Rifle:	Scope:	Ammo:
Rep 1 Best Dot: 2" / 1.5" / 1" / .75" / .5"			Supported / Sling	Support Type:
Rep 2 Best Dot: 2" / 1.5" / 1" / .75" / .5"		Rep 2 Score:		Total # of rounds out:
Rep 3 Best Dot: 2" / 1.5" / 1" / .75" / .5"		Rep 3 Score:		**Total Score:**
Notes:				

Date:	Location:	Rifle:	Scope:	Ammo:
Rep 1 Best Dot: 2" / 1.5" / 1" / .75" / .5"			Supported / Sling	Support Type:
Rep 2 Best Dot: 2" / 1.5" / 1" / .75" / .5"		Rep 2 Score:		Total # of rounds out:
Rep 3 Best Dot: 2" / 1.5" / 1" / .75" / .5"		Rep 3 Score:		**Total Score:**
Notes:				

Date:	Location:	Rifle:	Scope:	Ammo:
Rep 1 Best Dot: 2" / 1.5" / 1" / .75" / .5"			Supported / Sling	Support Type:
Rep 2 Best Dot: 2" / 1.5" / 1" / .75" / .5"		Rep 2 Score:		Total # of rounds out:
Rep 3 Best Dot: 2" / 1.5" / 1" / .75" / .5"		Rep 3 Score:		**Total Score:**
Notes:				

Accuracy Drill - 3

Precision Rifle ©

KNOW YOUR PRONE LIMITS

Date:		Location:				Rifle:		Scope:		Ammo:	
Rep 1 Best Dot:	2"	/ 1.5"	/ 1"	/ .75"	/ .5"			Supported / Sling		Support Type:	
Rep 2 Best Dot:	2"	/ 1.5"	/ 1"	/ .75"	/ .5"	Rep 2 Score:				Total # of rounds out:	
Rep 3 Best Dot:	2"	/ 1.5"	/ 1"	/ .75"	/ .5"	Rep 3 Score:				**Total Score:**	
Notes:											

Date:		Location:				Rifle:		Scope:		Ammo:	
Rep 1 Best Dot:	2"	/ 1.5"	/ 1"	/ .75"	/ .5"			Supported / Sling		Support Type:	
Rep 2 Best Dot:	2"	/ 1.5"	/ 1"	/ .75"	/ .5"	Rep 2 Score:				Total # of rounds out:	
Rep 3 Best Dot:	2"	/ 1.5"	/ 1"	/ .75"	/ .5"	Rep 3 Score:				**Total Score:**	
Notes:											

Date:		Location:				Rifle:		Scope:		Ammo:	
Rep 1 Best Dot:	2"	/ 1.5"	/ 1"	/ .75"	/ .5"			Supported / Sling		Support Type:	
Rep 2 Best Dot:	2"	/ 1.5"	/ 1"	/ .75"	/ .5"	Rep 2 Score:				Total # of rounds out:	
Rep 3 Best Dot:	2"	/ 1.5"	/ 1"	/ .75"	/ .5"	Rep 3 Score:				**Total Score:**	
Notes:											

KNOW YOUR PRONE LIMITS

◯ ◯ ◯ ◯ ○   ◯ ◯ ◯ ◯ ○   ◯ ◯ ◯ ◯ ○
◯ ◯ ◯ ◯ ○   ◯ ◯ ◯ ◯ ○   ◯ ◯ ◯ ◯ ○
◯ ◯ ◯ ◯ ○   ◯ ◯ ◯ ◯ ○   ◯ ◯ ◯ ◯ ○

Date:	Location:	Rifle:	Scope:	Ammo:
Rep 1 Best Dot:	2" / 1.5" / 1" / .75" / .5"		Supported / Sling	Support Type:
Rep 2 Best Dot:	2" / 1.5" / 1" / .75" / .5"	Rep 2 Score:		Total # of rounds out:
Rep 3 Best Dot:	2" / 1.5" / 1" / .75" / .5"	Rep 3 Score:		**Total Score:**
Notes:				

Date:	Location:	Rifle:	Scope:	Ammo:
Rep 1 Best Dot:	2" / 1.5" / 1" / .75" / .5"		Supported / Sling	Support Type:
Rep 2 Best Dot:	2" / 1.5" / 1" / .75" / .5"	Rep 2 Score:		Total # of rounds out:
Rep 3 Best Dot:	2" / 1.5" / 1" / .75" / .5"	Rep 3 Score:		**Total Score:**
Notes:				

Date:	Location:	Rifle:	Scope:	Ammo:
Rep 1 Best Dot:	2" / 1.5" / 1" / .75" / .5"		Supported / Sling	Support Type:
Rep 2 Best Dot:	2" / 1.5" / 1" / .75" / .5"	Rep 2 Score:		Total # of rounds out:
Rep 3 Best Dot:	2" / 1.5" / 1" / .75" / .5"	Rep 3 Score:		**Total Score:**
Notes:				

Accuracy Drill - 3

Precision Rifle ©

HOSTAGE

Purpose: Accuracy, stress, weapons handling.

Distance: 100 Yards to ?

Target: Cardboard IPSC targets X 2, with overlapping hostage target (attach a picture of your loved one).

Total Rounds Fired: ? Rounds.

Starting Position & Condition: Standing. Condition 1.

Description: Starting at 100 yards standing behind your rifle, assume a good prone shooting position and fire 1 round into the into the 5 point head A zone box of the limited visibility (bad guy) target. If successful, move 25 yards back and repeat the drill. Continue this drill until you miss or hit the hostage. Record your max accurate life saving distance.

Goals: Novice: 100 yards.   Expert: 200 yards.   Gunfighter: 300+ yards.

Variations:

- Add a 20 second time restraint.
- Any position except prone.

www.GUNFIGHTERSERIES.com ©

HOSTAGE

Date:	Location:	Rifle:	Ammo:	Notes:
20 Sec Par Time: Y / N	Shooting Position:		Max Distance:	
Date:	Location:	Rifle:	Ammo:	Notes:
20 Sec Par Time: Y / N	Shooting Position:		Max Distance:	
Date:	Location:	Rifle:	Ammo:	Notes:
20 Sec Par Time: Y / N	Shooting Position:		Max Distance:	
Date:	Location:	Rifle:	Ammo:	Notes:
20 Sec Par Time: Y / N	Shooting Position:		Max Distance:	
Date:	Location:	Rifle:	Ammo:	Notes:
20 Sec Par Time: Y / N	Shooting Position:		Max Distance:	
Date:	Location:	Rifle:	Ammo:	Notes:
20 Sec Par Time: Y / N	Shooting Position:		Max Distance:	
Date:	Location:	Rifle:	Ammo:	Notes:
20 Sec Par Time: Y / N	Shooting Position:		Max Distance:	
Date:	Location:	Rifle:	Ammo:	Notes:
20 Sec Par Time: Y / N	Shooting Position:		Max Distance:	
Date:	Location:	Rifle:	Ammo:	Notes:
20 Sec Par Time: Y / N	Shooting Position:		Max Distance:	
Date:	Location:	Rifle:	Ammo:	Notes:
20 Sec Par Time: Y / N	Shooting Position:		Max Distance:	

Accuracy Drill - 4

Precision Rifle ©

HOSTAGE

Date:	Location:	Rifle:	Ammo:	Notes:
20 Sec Par Time: Y / N	Shooting Position:		Max Distance:	
Date:	Location:	Rifle:	Ammo:	Notes:
20 Sec Par Time: Y / N	Shooting Position:		Max Distance:	
Date:	Location:	Rifle:	Ammo:	Notes:
20 Sec Par Time: Y / N	Shooting Position:		Max Distance:	
Date:	Location:	Rifle:	Ammo:	Notes:
20 Sec Par Time: Y / N	Shooting Position:		Max Distance:	
Date:	Location:	Rifle:	Ammo:	Notes:
20 Sec Par Time: Y / N	Shooting Position:		Max Distance:	
Date:	Location:	Rifle:	Ammo:	Notes:
20 Sec Par Time: Y / N	Shooting Position:		Max Distance:	
Date:	Location:	Rifle:	Ammo:	Notes:
20 Sec Par Time: Y / N	Shooting Position:		Max Distance:	
Date:	Location:	Rifle:	Ammo:	Notes:
20 Sec Par Time: Y / N	Shooting Position:		Max Distance:	
Date:	Location:	Rifle:	Ammo:	Notes:
20 Sec Par Time: Y / N	Shooting Position:		Max Distance:	
Date:	Location:	Rifle:	Ammo:	Notes:
20 Sec Par Time: Y / N	Shooting Position:		Max Distance:	

www.GUNFIGHTERSERIES.com ©

HOSTAGE

Date:	Location:	Rifle:	Ammo:	Notes:
20 Sec Par Time: Y / N	Shooting Position:		Max Distance:	
Date:	Location:	Rifle:	Ammo:	Notes:
20 Sec Par Time: Y / N	Shooting Position:		Max Distance:	
Date:	Location:	Rifle:	Ammo:	Notes:
20 Sec Par Time: Y / N	Shooting Position:		Max Distance:	
Date:	Location:	Rifle:	Ammo:	Notes:
20 Sec Par Time: Y / N	Shooting Position:		Max Distance:	
Date:	Location:	Rifle:	Ammo:	Notes:
20 Sec Par Time: Y / N	Shooting Position:		Max Distance:	
Date:	Location:	Rifle:	Ammo:	Notes:
20 Sec Par Time: Y / N	Shooting Position:		Max Distance:	
Date:	Location:	Rifle:	Ammo:	Notes:
20 Sec Par Time: Y / N	Shooting Position:		Max Distance:	
Date:	Location:	Rifle:	Ammo:	Notes:
20 Sec Par Time: Y / N	Shooting Position:		Max Distance:	
Date:	Location:	Rifle:	Ammo:	Notes:
20 Sec Par Time: Y / N	Shooting Position:		Max Distance:	

Precision Rifle ©

Accuracy Drill - 4

HOSTAGE

Date:	Location:	Rifle:	Ammo:	Notes:
20 Sec Par Time: Y / N	Shooting Position:		Max Distance:	
Date:	Location:	Rifle:	Ammo:	Notes:
20 Sec Par Time: Y / N	Shooting Position:		Max Distance:	
Date:	Location:	Rifle:	Ammo:	Notes:
20 Sec Par Time: Y / N	Shooting Position:		Max Distance:	
Date:	Location:	Rifle:	Ammo:	Notes:
20 Sec Par Time: Y / N	Shooting Position:		Max Distance:	
Date:	Location:	Rifle:	Ammo:	Notes:
20 Sec Par Time: Y / N	Shooting Position:		Max Distance:	
Date:	Location:	Rifle:	Ammo:	Notes:
20 Sec Par Time: Y / N	Shooting Position:		Max Distance:	
Date:	Location:	Rifle:	Ammo:	Notes:
20 Sec Par Time: Y / N	Shooting Position:		Max Distance:	
Date:	Location:	Rifle:	Ammo:	Notes:
20 Sec Par Time: Y / N	Shooting Position:		Max Distance:	
Date:	Location:	Rifle:	Ammo:	Notes:
20 Sec Par Time: Y / N	Shooting Position:		Max Distance:	
Date:	Location:	Rifle:	Ammo:	Notes:
20 Sec Par Time: Y / N	Shooting Position:		Max Distance:	

www.GUNFIGHTERSERIES.com ©

HOSTAGE

Date:	Location:	Rifle:	Ammo:	Notes:
20 Sec Par Time: Y / N	Shooting Position:		Max Distance:	
Date:	Location:	Rifle:	Ammo:	Notes:
20 Sec Par Time: Y / N	Shooting Position:		Max Distance:	
Date:	Location:	Rifle:	Ammo:	Notes:
20 Sec Par Time: Y / N	Shooting Position:		Max Distance:	
Date:	Location:	Rifle:	Ammo:	Notes:
20 Sec Par Time: Y / N	Shooting Position:		Max Distance:	
Date:	Location:	Rifle:	Ammo:	Notes:
20 Sec Par Time: Y / N	Shooting Position:		Max Distance:	
Date:	Location:	Rifle:	Ammo:	Notes:
20 Sec Par Time: Y / N	Shooting Position:		Max Distance:	
Date:	Location:	Rifle:	Ammo:	Notes:
20 Sec Par Time: Y / N	Shooting Position:		Max Distance:	
Date:	Location:	Rifle:	Ammo:	Notes:
20 Sec Par Time: Y / N	Shooting Position:		Max Distance:	
Date:	Location:	Rifle:	Ammo:	Notes:
20 Sec Par Time: Y / N	Shooting Position:		Max Distance:	

Accuracy Drill - 4

THE RECOIL GAME

Purpose: Reinforce follow-through, spotting trace and impact for quick corrections to follow-up shots.

By: Francis Colon.

Distance: 500 Yards.

Target: Steel circle, or head silhouette, targets no larger than 8 inches.

Extra Equipment Needed: Spotting scope, shooting partner and shot timer.

Par Time: Per goal standard.

Rounds Fired Per Rep: 3 Rounds.

Total Rounds Fired: 9 Rounds.

Point Penalty: 1 Point per impact. (1st round of each rep does not count for points.)

Repetitions: 3 Reps.

Starting Position & Condition: Prone. Condition 1.

Description: Start in a solid prone shooting position aimed in on target, scope turrets dialed for proper firing solution, then close your eyes.

Have your shooting partner turn your elevation and/or windage turrets +/- 10 clicks (Mil or MOA doesn't matter). Your partner will start the timer when ready to observe.

At the timer beep, open your eyes, without looking at your turrets, fire one spotter round at your target. With a good shooting position and proper follow-through you will observe your own trace and impact splash. Using your reticle, measure the distance of your impact from center of target, make a correction by offset aiming and quickly fire 2 more shots for score.

Goals: Novice: 20 Seconds with at least 1 point per rep.   Expert: 15 Seconds with 2 points per rep.   Gunfighter: 8 Seconds with 2 points per rep.

Variations:

Use a smaller target at a different range. Very difficult closer than 300 yards or further than 800 yards.

Use a target without a backstop berm.

www.GUNFIGHTERSERIES.com ©

THE RECOIL GAME

	Rep 1	Rep 2	Rep 3
	◯	◯	◯
	◯	◯	◯
	◯	◯	◯
	◯	◯	◯
	◯	◯	◯

Date:	Rifle:	Scope:
Rep 1: Time	Rep 2: Time	Rep 3: Time
Rep 1: Score	Rep 2: Score	Rep 3: Score
Notes:		**Total Score:**

Date:	Rifle:	Scope:
Rep 1: Time	Rep 2: Time	Rep 3: Time
Rep 1: Score	Rep 2: Score	Rep 3: Score
Notes:		**Total Score:**

Date:	Rifle:	Scope:
Rep 1: Time	Rep 2: Time	Rep 3: Time
Rep 1: Score	Rep 2: Score	Rep 3: Score
Notes:		**Total Score:**

Date:	Rifle:	Scope:
Rep 1: Time	Rep 2: Time	Rep 3: Time
Rep 1: Score	Rep 2: Score	Rep 3: Score
Notes:		**Total Score:**

Date:	Rifle:	Scope:
Rep 1: Time	Rep 2: Time	Rep 3: Time
Rep 1: Score	Rep 2: Score	Rep 3: Score
Notes:		**Total Score:**

Accuracy Drill - 5

THE RECOIL GAME

www.GUNFIGHTERSERIES.com ©

Rep 1 Rep 2 Rep 3

Date:	Rifle:	Scope:
Rep 1: Time	Rep 2: Time	Rep 3: Time
Rep 1: Score	Rep 2: Score	Rep 3: Score
Notes:		Total Score:

Date:	Rifle:	Scope:
Rep 1: Time	Rep 2: Time	Rep 3: Time
Rep 1: Score	Rep 2: Score	Rep 3: Score
Notes:		Total Score:

Date:	Rifle:	Scope:
Rep 1: Time	Rep 2: Time	Rep 3: Time
Rep 1: Score	Rep 2: Score	Rep 3: Score
Notes:		Total Score:

Date:	Rifle:	Scope:
Rep 1: Time	Rep 2: Time	Rep 3: Time
Rep 1: Score	Rep 2: Score	Rep 3: Score
Notes:		Total Score:

Date:	Rifle:	Scope:
Rep 1: Time	Rep 2: Time	Rep 3: Time
Rep 1: Score	Rep 2: Score	Rep 3: Score
Notes:		Total Score:

THE RECOIL GAME

Rep 1   Rep 2   Rep 3

Date:	Rifle:	Scope:
Rep 1: Time	Rep 2: Time	Rep 3: Time
Rep 1: Score	Rep 2: Score	Rep 3: Score
Notes:		Total Score:

Date:	Rifle:	Scope:
Rep 1: Time	Rep 2: Time	Rep 3: Time
Rep 1: Score	Rep 2: Score	Rep 3: Score
Notes:		Total Score:

Date:	Rifle:	Scope:
Rep 1: Time	Rep 2: Time	Rep 3: Time
Rep 1: Score	Rep 2: Score	Rep 3: Score
Notes:		Total Score:

Date:	Rifle:	Scope:
Rep 1: Time	Rep 2: Time	Rep 3: Time
Rep 1: Score	Rep 2: Score	Rep 3: Score
Notes:		Total Score:

Date:	Rifle:	Scope:
Rep 1: Time	Rep 2: Time	Rep 3: Time
Rep 1: Score	Rep 2: Score	Rep 3: Score
Notes:		Total Score:

Accuracy Drill - 5

Precision Rifle ©

THE RECOIL GAME

Rep 1	Rep 2	Rep 3
○	○	○
○	○	○
○	○	○
○	○	○
○	○	○

Date:	Rifle:	Scope:
Rep 1: Time	Rep 2: Time	Rep 3: Time
Rep 1: Score	Rep 2: Score	Rep 3: Score
Notes:		Total Score:

Date:	Rifle:	Scope:
Rep 1: Time	Rep 2: Time	Rep 3: Time
Rep 1: Score	Rep 2: Score	Rep 3: Score
Notes:		Total Score:

Date:	Rifle:	Scope:
Rep 1: Time	Rep 2: Time	Rep 3: Time
Rep 1: Score	Rep 2: Score	Rep 3: Score
Notes:		Total Score:

Date:	Rifle:	Scope:
Rep 1: Time	Rep 2: Time	Rep 3: Time
Rep 1: Score	Rep 2: Score	Rep 3: Score
Notes:		Total Score:

Date:	Rifle:	Scope:
Rep 1: Time	Rep 2: Time	Rep 3: Time
Rep 1: Score	Rep 2: Score	Rep 3: Score
Notes:		Total Score:

www.GUNFIGHTERSERIES.com ©

THE RECOIL GAME

			Rep 1	Rep 2	Rep 3
Date:	Rifle:	Scope:	○	○	○
Rep 1: Time	Rep 2: Time	Rep 3: Time			
Rep 1: Score	Rep 2: Score	Rep 3: Score			
Notes:		Total Score:			
Date:	Rifle:	Scope:	○	○	○
Rep 1: Time	Rep 2: Time	Rep 3: Time			
Rep 1: Score	Rep 2: Score	Rep 3: Score			
Notes:		Total Score:			
Date:	Rifle:	Scope:	○	○	○
Rep 1: Time	Rep 2: Time	Rep 3: Time			
Rep 1: Score	Rep 2: Score	Rep 3: Score			
Notes:		Total Score:			
Date:	Rifle:	Scope:	○	○	○
Rep 1: Time	Rep 2: Time	Rep 3: Time			
Rep 1: Score	Rep 2: Score	Rep 3: Score			
Notes:		Total Score:			
Date:	Rifle:	Scope:	○	○	○
Rep 1: Time	Rep 2: Time	Rep 3: Time			
Rep 1: Score	Rep 2: Score	Rep 3: Score			
Notes:		Total Score:			

Precision Rifle ©

Accuracy Drill - 5

RANGE ESTIMATION

Purpose: To become more proficient with range estimating without electronics.

Distance: 300 to 800 yards.

Target: Known size steel.

Extra Equipment Needed: Spotting scope, shooting partner and Laser Range Finder.

Total Rounds Fired: 8 Rounds.

Point Penalty: Hit / Miss.

Starting Position & Condition: Prone. Condition 4.

Description: Identify 8 unknown distance targets between 300 to 800 yards. Assume a good observation position; prone being the most stable and tactical. With your eyes only (no additional tools), record your best guess distance to each target. Next use the MOA or Mil reticle of your rifle or spotting scope to measure and calculate the distance to each target. To confirm your accuracy adjust your scope elevation for the range that you estimated and fire one round at each target. Next, confirm and calculate your percentage of error using a LRF (Laser Range Finder).

Estimate by Eye Goals: Novice: +/- 30% of true range. Expert: +/- 20% of true range. Gunfighter: +/- 15% of true range.

Estimate with Reticle Goals: Novice: +/- 15% of true range. Expert: +/- 10% of true range. Gunfighter: +/- 5% of true range.

RANGE ESTIMATION WORKSHEET

Date:		Location:		Rifle:		Scope:		Ammo:	
Target 1	Est Range by Eye: _____ Yards	SOT in Inches: _____	X 27.77 (Mils) or 95.5 (MOA)	Est. Range: _____ Yards		Live Fire: Hit / Miss			
		Divide by SOT in MOA or MIL: _____		Elevation: _____		LRF Range: _____ Yards			
Target 2	Est Range by Eye: _____ Yards	SOT in Inches: _____	X 27.77 (Mils) or 95.5 (MOA)	Est. Range: _____ Yards		Live Fire: Hit / Miss			
		Divide by SOT in MOA or MIL: _____		Elevation: _____		LRF Range: _____ Yards			
Target 3	Est Range by Eye: _____ Yards	SOT in Inches: _____	X 27.77 (Mils) or 95.5 (MOA)	Est. Range: _____ Yards		Live Fire: Hit / Miss			
		Divide by SOT in MOA or MIL: _____		Elevation: _____		LRF Range: _____ Yards			
Target 4	Est Range by Eye: _____ Yards	SOT in Inches: _____	X 27.77 (Mils) or 95.5 (MOA)	Est. Range: _____ Yards		Live Fire: Hit / Miss			
		Divide by SOT in MOA or MIL: _____		Elevation: _____		LRF Range: _____ Yards			
Target 5	Est Range by Eye: _____ Yards	SOT in Inches: _____	X 27.77 (Mils) or 95.5 (MOA)	Est. Range: _____ Yards		Live Fire: Hit / Miss			
		Divide by SOT in MOA or MIL: _____		Elevation: _____		LRF Range: _____ Yards			
Target 6	Est Range by Eye: _____ Yards	SOT in Inches: _____	X 27.77 (Mils) or 95.5 (MOA)	Est. Range: _____ Yards		Live Fire: Hit / Miss			
		Divide by SOT in MOA or MIL: _____		Elevation: _____		LRF Range: _____ Yards			
Target 7	Est Range by Eye: _____ Yards	SOT in Inches: _____	X 27.77 (Mils) or 95.5 (MOA)	Est. Range: _____ Yards		Live Fire: Hit / Miss			
		Divide by SOT in MOA or MIL: _____		Elevation: _____		LRF Range: _____ Yards			
Target 8	Est Range by Eye: _____ Yards	SOT in Inches: _____	X 27.77 (Mils) or 95.5 (MOA)	Est. Range: _____ Yards		Live Fire: Hit / Miss			
		Divide by SOT in MOA or MIL: _____		Elevation: _____		LRF Range: _____ Yards			

Range Estimation

Precision Rifle ©

RANGE ESTIMATION WORKSHEET

Date:	Location:	Rifle:	Scope:	Ammo:
Target 1	Est Range by Eye: _____ Yards	SOT in Inches: _____ X 27.77 (Mils) or 95.5 (MOA) Divide by SOT in MOA or MIL: _____	Est. Range: _____ Yards Elevation:	Live Fire: Hit / Miss LRF Range: _____ Yards
Target 2	Est Range by Eye: _____ Yards	SOT in Inches: _____ X 27.77 (Mils) or 95.5 (MOA) Divide by SOT in MOA or MIL: _____	Est. Range: _____ Yards Elevation:	Live Fire: Hit / Miss LRF Range: _____ Yards
Target 3	Est Range by Eye: _____ Yards	SOT in Inches: _____ X 27.77 (Mils) or 95.5 (MOA) Divide by SOT in MOA or MIL: _____	Est. Range: _____ Yards Elevation:	Live Fire: Hit / Miss LRF Range: _____ Yards
Target 4	Est Range by Eye: _____ Yards	SOT in Inches: _____ X 27.77 (Mils) or 95.5 (MOA) Divide by SOT in MOA or MIL: _____	Est. Range: _____ Yards Elevation:	Live Fire: Hit / Miss LRF Range: _____ Yards
Target 5	Est Range by Eye: _____ Yards	SOT in Inches: _____ X 27.77 (Mils) or 95.5 (MOA) Divide by SOT in MOA or MIL: _____	Est. Range: _____ Yards Elevation:	Live Fire: Hit / Miss LRF Range: _____ Yards
Target 6	Est Range by Eye: _____ Yards	SOT in Inches: _____ X 27.77 (Mils) or 95.5 (MOA) Divide by SOT in MOA or MIL: _____	Est. Range: _____ Yards Elevation:	Live Fire: Hit / Miss LRF Range: _____ Yards
Target 7	Est Range by Eye: _____ Yards	SOT in Inches: _____ X 27.77 (Mils) or 95.5 (MOA) Divide by SOT in MOA or MIL: _____	Est. Range: _____ Yards Elevation:	Live Fire: Hit / Miss LRF Range: _____ Yards
Target 8	Est Range by Eye: _____ Yards	SOT in Inches: _____ X 27.77 (Mils) or 95.5 (MOA) Divide by SOT in MOA or MIL: _____	Est. Range: _____ Yards Elevation:	Live Fire: Hit / Miss LRF Range: _____ Yards

RANGE ESTIMATION WORKSHEET

Date:	Location:	Rifle:	Scope:	Ammo:
Target 1	Est Range by Eye: _____ Yards	SOT in Inches: _____ X 27.77 (Mils) or 95.5 (MOA) Divide by SOT in MOA or MIL: _____	Est. Range: _____ Yards Elevation:	Live Fire: Hit / Miss LRF Range: _____ Yards
Target 2	Est Range by Eye: _____ Yards	SOT in Inches: _____ X 27.77 (Mils) or 95.5 (MOA) Divide by SOT in MOA or MIL: _____	Est. Range: _____ Yards Elevation:	Live Fire: Hit / Miss LRF Range: _____ Yards
Target 3	Est Range by Eye: _____ Yards	SOT in Inches: _____ X 27.77 (Mils) or 95.5 (MOA) Divide by SOT in MOA or MIL: _____	Est. Range: _____ Yards Elevation:	Live Fire: Hit / Miss LRF Range: _____ Yards
Target 4	Est Range by Eye: _____ Yards	SOT in Inches: _____ X 27.77 (Mils) or 95.5 (MOA) Divide by SOT in MOA or MIL: _____	Est. Range: _____ Yards Elevation:	Live Fire: Hit / Miss LRF Range: _____ Yards
Target 5	Est Range by Eye: _____ Yards	SOT in Inches: _____ X 27.77 (Mils) or 95.5 (MOA) Divide by SOT in MOA or MIL: _____	Est. Range: _____ Yards Elevation:	Live Fire: Hit / Miss LRF Range: _____ Yards
Target 6	Est Range by Eye: _____ Yards	SOT in Inches: _____ X 27.77 (Mils) or 95.5 (MOA) Divide by SOT in MOA or MIL: _____	Est. Range: _____ Yards Elevation:	Live Fire: Hit / Miss LRF Range: _____ Yards
Target 7	Est Range by Eye: _____ Yards	SOT in Inches: _____ X 27.77 (Mils) or 95.5 (MOA) Divide by SOT in MOA or MIL: _____	Est. Range: _____ Yards Elevation:	Live Fire: Hit / Miss LRF Range: _____ Yards
Target 8	Est Range by Eye: _____ Yards	SOT in Inches: _____ X 27.77 (Mils) or 95.5 (MOA) Divide by SOT in MOA or MIL: _____	Est. Range: _____ Yards Elevation:	Live Fire: Hit / Miss LRF Range: _____ Yards

Precision Rifle ©

Range Estimation

RANGE ESTIMATION WORKSHEET

www.GUNFIGHTERSERIES.com ©

Date:	Location:	Rifle:	Scope.	Ammo:
Target 1	Est Range by Eye: _____ Yards	SOT in Inches: _____ X 27.77 (Mils) or 95.5 (MOA) Divide by SOT in MOA or MIL: _____	Est. Range: _____ Yards Elevation:	Live Fire: Hit / Miss LRF Range: _____ Yards
Target 2	Est Range by Eye: _____ Yards	SOT in Inches: _____ X 27.77 (Mils) or 95.5 (MOA) Divide by SOT in MOA or MIL: _____	Est. Range: _____ Yards Elevation:	Live Fire: Hit / Miss LRF Range: _____ Yards
Target 3	Est Range by Eye: _____ Yards	SOT in Inches: _____ X 27.77 (Mils) or 95.5 (MOA) Divide by SOT in MOA or MIL: _____	Est. Range: _____ Yards Elevation:	Live Fire: Hit / Miss LRF Range: _____ Yards
Target 4	Est Range by Eye: _____ Yards	SOT in Inches: _____ X 27.77 (Mils) or 95.5 (MOA) Divide by SOT in MOA or MIL: _____	Est. Range: _____ Yards Elevation:	Live Fire: Hit / Miss LRF Range: _____ Yards
Target 5	Est Range by Eye: _____ Yards	SOT in Inches: _____ X 27.77 (Mils) or 95.5 (MOA) Divide by SOT in MOA or MIL: _____	Est. Range: _____ Yards Elevation:	Live Fire: Hit / Miss LRF Range: _____ Yards
Target 6	Est Range by Eye: _____ Yards	SOT in Inches: _____ X 27.77 (Mils) or 95.5 (MOA) Divide by SOT in MOA or MIL: _____	Est. Range: _____ Yards Elevation:	Live Fire: Hit / Miss LRF Range: _____ Yards
Target 7	Est Range by Eye: _____ Yards	SOT in Inches: _____ X 27.77 (Mils) or 95.5 (MOA) Divide by SOT in MOA or MIL: _____	Est. Range: _____ Yards Elevation:	Live Fire: Hit / Miss LRF Range: _____ Yards
Target 8	Est Range by Eye: _____ Yards	SOT in Inches: _____ X 27.77 (Mils) or 95.5 (MOA) Divide by SOT in MOA or MIL: _____	Est. Range: _____ Yards Elevation:	Live Fire: Hit / Miss LRF Range: _____ Yards

RANGE ESTIMATION WORKSHEET

Date:		Location:		Rifle:		Scope.		Ammo:	
Target 1	Est Range by Eye: _____ Yards	SOT in Inches: _____ Divide by SOT in MOA or MIL: _____	X 27.77 (Mils) or 95.5 (MOA)			Est. Range: _____ Yards		Live Fire: Hit / Miss	
						Elevation:		LRF Range: _____ Yards	
Target 2	Est Range by Eye: _____ Yards	SOT in Inches: _____ Divide by SOT in MOA or MIL: _____	X 27.77 (Mils) or 95.5 (MOA)			Est. Range: _____ Yards		Live Fire: Hit / Miss	
						Elevation:		LRF Range: _____ Yards	
Target 3	Est Range by Eye: _____ Yards	SOT in Inches: _____ Divide by SOT in MOA or MIL: _____	X 27.77 (Mils) or 95.5 (MOA)			Est. Range: _____ Yards		Live Fire: Hit / Miss	
						Elevation:		LRF Range: _____ Yards	
Target 4	Est Range by Eye: _____ Yards	SOT in Inches: _____ Divide by SOT in MOA or MIL: _____	X 27.77 (Mils) or 95.5 (MOA)			Est. Range: _____ Yards		Live Fire: Hit / Miss	
						Elevation:		LRF Range: _____ Yards	
Target 5	Est Range by Eye: _____ Yards	SOT in Inches: _____ Divide by SOT in MOA or MIL: _____	X 27.77 (Mils) or 95.5 (MOA)			Est. Range: _____ Yards		Live Fire: Hit / Miss	
						Elevation:		LRF Range: _____ Yards	
Target 6	Est Range by Eye: _____ Yards	SOT in Inches: _____ Divide by SOT in MOA or MIL: _____	X 27.77 (Mils) or 95.5 (MOA)			Est. Range: _____ Yards		Live Fire: Hit / Miss	
						Elevation:		LRF Range: _____ Yards	
Target 7	Est Range by Eye: _____ Yards	SOT in Inches: _____ Divide by SOT in MOA or MIL: _____	X 27.77 (Mils) or 95.5 (MOA)			Est. Range: _____ Yards		Live Fire: Hit / Miss	
						Elevation:		LRF Range: _____ Yards	
Target 8	Est Range by Eye: _____ Yards	SOT in Inches: _____ Divide by SOT in MOA or MIL: _____	X 27.77 (Mils) or 95.5 (MOA)			Est. Range: _____ Yards		Live Fire: Hit / Miss	
						Elevation:		LRF Range: _____ Yards	

Range Estimation

Precision Rifle ©

WIND ARC

Purpose: To become more proficient compensating for wind effects on you bullet.

Extra Equipment Needed: Ballistics calculator / chart for grading.

Starting Position & Condition: Any. Condition 4.

Description: Fill in a wind arc to the best of your ability without the aid or references of a ballistics chart or calculator.

Start by filling in a notional random range to target (any distance greater than 300 yards / meters). Next fill in each "WIND EFFECT IN INCHES" bubble on the left side of the wind arc with how much deviation from center is caused by the wind. Each "WIND EFFECT" bubble corresponds with a 5, 10, 15, 20, and 25 MPH wind speeds at a 30, 60 and 90 degrees wind direction.

Next, fill in each "ADJUSTMENT" bubble in your popper unit of measurement (Mil or MOA) needed to compensate for the reference wind deviation from center.

Once completed, use your ballistics chart and/or ballistics calculator to grade your wind arc.

Goals:

Novice: Within 1 MOA or 0.3 Mil.

Expert: Within 0.5 MOA or 0.2 Mil.

Gunfighter: Within 0.25 MOA or 0.1 Mil.

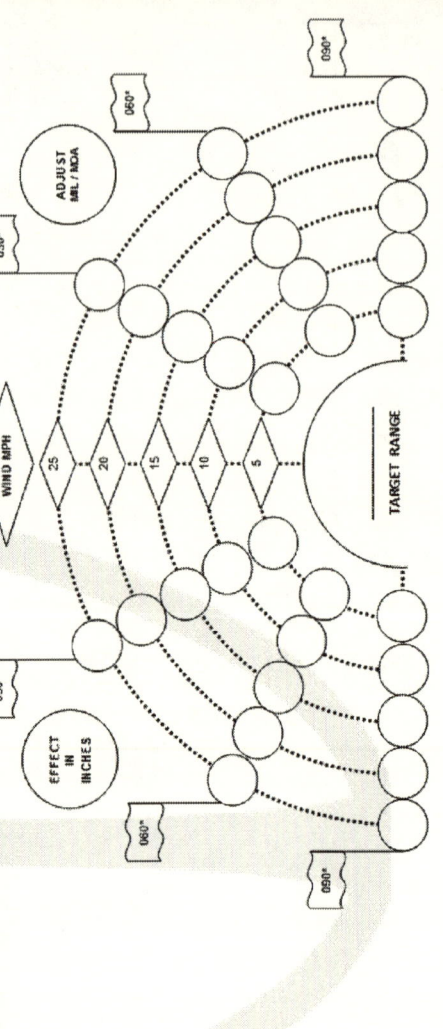

Wind Estimation Drills - 1

Rifle:
Ammo:
MV:
Temp:
Baro:

WIND MPH: 25 | 20 | 15 | 10 | 5

TARGET RANGE

EFFECT IN INCHES

ADJUST MIL / MOA

030° | 060° | 090°

Precision Rifle ©

www.GUNFIGHTERSERIES.com ©

Rifle:
Ammo:
MV:
Temp:
Baro:

WIND MPH: 25, 20, 15, 10, 5

ADJUST MIL / MOA

EFFECT IN INCHES

TARGET RANGE

030*, 060*, 090* (upper)
030*, 060*, 090* (lower)

Wind Estimation Drills - 1

WIND MPH: 25, 20, 15, 10, 5

ADJUST MIL / MOA

EFFECT IN INCHES

TARGET RANGE

Angles: 030*, 060*, 090*

Rifle:
Ammo:
MV:
Temp:
Baro:

Precision Rifle ©

Rifle: _____
Ammo: _____
MV: _____
Temp: _____
Baro: _____

www.GUNFIGHTERSERIES.com ©

WIND MPH: 25, 20, 15, 10, 5

ADJUST MIL / MOA

EFFECT IN INCHES

TARGET RANGE

030° · 060° · 090°
030° · 060° · 090°

Rifle:
Ammo:
MV:
Temp:
Baro:

WIND MPH: 25, 20, 15, 10, 5

ADJUST MIL / MOA

EFFECT IN INCHES

TARGET RANGE

030° | 060° | 090°

Wind Estimation Drills - 1

Precision Rifle ©

WIND READING

Purpose: To become more proficient with estimating wind speeds.

Distance: Minimum of 500 Yards.

Target: Known distance and known size steel. Unless you have KD pit service available.

Extra Equipment Needed: Wind flags, spotting scope, shooting partner.

Rounds Fired Per Rep: 1 Round. **Total Rounds Fired:** 3 Rounds.

Starting Position & Condition: Prone. Condition 1.

Description: Record current temperature, range to target and elevation adjustment needed. Be sure your elevation DOPE is correct, because this exercise focuses entirely on left & right corrections only.

    Using Wind Flags: First identify if you are observing a cotton or nylon flag, the weight and material makes a difference. Observe and record angle of the flag, the direction and the value. Make a wind speed estimate and correction based on your estimate.

    Using Environmental: Observe and record the wind effects in your area. Observe and record the direction and value. Make a wind speed estimate and correction based on your estimate.

    Using Mirage: Observe and record the direction the mirage is flowing and at which angle. If possible observe and record the direction and value. Make a wind speed estimate and correction based on your estimate.

After making an estimated wind speed and correction: Fire one round center mass then record the distance left or right of center. Record what the true correction should have been and also the true wind speed based off the impact.

Goals: Novice: Impact within 2 MOA or 0.6 Mil.   Expert: Impact within 1 MOA or 0.4 Mil.   Gunfighter: Impact within 1/2 MOA or 0.2 Mil.

www.gunfighterseries.com ©

WIND READING WORKSHEET (Flags)

○ ○ ○ ○

Date:	Location:		Rifle		Scope:	
Ammo:	Temp:	Baro:	Distance:		Elev:	
Flag Type: Nylon / Cotton	Est Speed:	MPH	Value: Full 3/4 1/2 1/4 0		Est: Correction:	L / R
Angle: 15* 30* 45* 60* 75* 90*	Distance From Center:		True Speed:	MPH	True Correction:	
Date:	Location:		Rifle		Scope:	
Ammo:	Temp:	Baro:	Distance:		Elev:	
Flag Type: Nylon / Cotton	Est Speed:	MPH	Value: Full 3/4 1/2 1/4 0		Est: Correction:	L / R
Angle: 15* 30* 45* 60* 75* 90*	Distance From Center:		True Speed:	MPH	True Correction:	
Date:	Location:		Rifle		Scope:	
Ammo:	Temp:	Baro:	Distance:		Elev:	
Flag Type: Nylon / Cotton	Est Speed:	MPH	Value: Full 3/4 1/2 1/4 0		Est: Correction:	L / R
Angle: 15* 30* 45* 60* 75* 90*	Distance From Center:		True Speed:	MPH	True Correction:	
Date:	Location:		Rifle		Scope:	
Ammo:	Temp:	Baro:	Distance:		Elev:	
Flag Type: Nylon / Cotton	Est Speed:	MPH	Value: Full 3/4 1/2 1/4 0		Est: Correction:	L / R
Angle: 15* 30* 45* 60* 75* 90*	Distance From Center:		True Speed:		MPH True Correction:	

Wind Estimation Drills - 2

Precision Rifle ©

WIND READING WORKSHEET (Flags)

Date:	Location:		Rifle		Scope:	
Ammo:	Temp:	Baro:	Distance:		Elev:	
	Est Speed:	MPH	Value: Full 3/4 1/2 1/4 0		Est: Correction:	L / R
Flag Type: Nylon / Cotton	Distance From Center:		True Speed:	MPH	True Correction:	
Angle: 15* 30* 45* 60* 75* 90*						
Date:	Location:		Rifle		Scope:	
Ammo:	Temp:	Baro:	Distance:		Elev:	
	Est Speed:	MPH	Value: Full 3/4 1/2 1/4 0		Est: Correction:	L / R
Flag Type: Nylon / Cotton	Distance From Center:		True Speed:	MPH	True Correction:	
Angle: 15* 30* 45* 60* 75* 90*						
Date:	Location:		Rifle		Scope:	
Ammo:	Temp:	Baro:	Distance:		Elev:	
	Est Speed:	MPH	Value: Full 3/4 1/2 1/4 0		Est: Correction:	L / R
Flag Type: Nylon / Cotton	Distance From Center:		True Speed:	MPH	True Correction:	
Angle: 15* 30* 45* 60* 75* 90*						
Date:	Location:		Rifle		Scope:	
Ammo:	Temp:	Baro:	Distance:		Elev:	
	Est Speed:	MPH	Value: Full 3/4 1/2 1/4 0		Est: Correction:	L / R
Flag Type: Nylon / Cotton	Distance From Center:		True Speed:	MPH	True Correction:	
Angle: 15* 30* 45* 60* 75* 90*						

www.GUNFIGHTERSERIES.com ©

WIND READING WORKSHEET (Mirage)

Date:	Location:	Rifle	Scope:
Ammo:	Temp:	Baro:	Distance:	Elev:
Mirage Direction: L / R	Est Speed:	MPH	Value: Full 3/4 1/2 1/4 0	Est: Correction: L / R
Angle: 0 30* 45* 90*	Distance From Center:	True Speed: MPH	True Correction:

Date:	Location:	Rifle	Scope:
Ammo:	Temp:	Baro:	Distance:	Elev:
Mirage Direction: L / R	Est Speed:	MPH	Value: Full 3/4 1/2 1/4 0	Est: Correction: L / R
Angle: 0 30* 45* 90*	Distance From Center:	True Speed: MPH	True Correction:

Date:	Location:	Rifle	Scope:
Ammo:	Temp:	Baro:	Distance:	Elev:
Mirage Direction: L / R	Est Speed:	MPH	Value: Full 3/4 1/2 1/4 0	Est: Correction: L / R
Angle: 0 30* 45* 90*	Distance From Center:	True Speed: MPH	True Correction:

Date:	Location:	Rifle	Scope:
Ammo:	Temp:	Baro:	Distance:	Elev:
Mirage Direction: L / R	Est Speed:	MPH	Value: Full 3/4 1/2 1/4 0	Est: Correction: L / R
Angle: 0 30* 45* 90*	Distance From Center:	True Speed: MPH	True Correction:

Wind Estimation Drills - 2

Precision Rifle ©

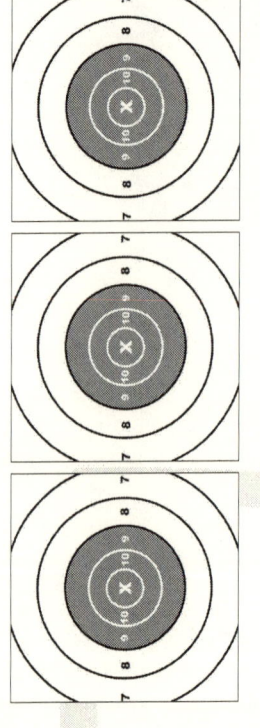

SIT, KNEEL, STAND (SLING)

Purpose: Increase sling proficiency and accuracy in multiple shooting positions.

Distance: 100 Yards.

Target: GF-2 X 3

Par Time: 2 Minutes per stage.

Extra Equipment Needed: Shot timer.

Rounds Fired Per Stage: 3 Rounds.   **Total Rounds Fired:** 9 Rounds.

Point Penalty: As per target score.

Repetitions: 1 Rep of 3 stages.

Starting Position & Condition: See description for position. Condition 1.

Description Sitting: Assume a good sitting position utilizing sling support only. At the timer beep, fire 3 rounds into the first target. Reload.

Description Kneeling: Assume a good kneeling position utilizing sling support. At the timer beep, fire 3 rounds into the second target. Reload.

Description Standing: Assume a good standing position utilizing sling support. At the timer beep, fire 3 rounds into the third target. Score targets.

Goals: Novice: 70 points under par.   Expert: 80 points under par.   Gunfighter: 90 points under par.

Variations: Start from a standing low ready position and give yourself a 45 second par time per 3 shot repetition.

SIT, KNEEL, STAND (SLING)

Date:	Rifle:	Scope:	Sling Used:	Notes:
Sitting Score:	Kneeling Score:	Standing Score:	**Total Score:**	

Date:	Rifle:	Scope:	Sling Used:	Notes:
Sitting Score:	Kneeling Score:	Standing Score:	**Total Score:**	

Date:	Rifle:	Scope:	Sling Used:	Notes:
Sitting Score:	Kneeling Score:	Standing Score:	**Total Score:**	

Date:	Rifle:	Scope:	Sling Used:	Notes:
Sitting Score:	Kneeling Score:	Standing Score:	**Total Score:**	

Date:	Rifle:	Scope:	Sling Used:	Notes:
Sitting Score:	Kneeling Score:	Standing Score:	**Total Score:**	

Position Drills - 1

Precision Rifle ©

SIT, KNEEL, STAND (SLING)

www.GUNFIGHTERSERIES.com ©

Date:	Rifle:	Scope:	Sling Used:	Notes:
Sitting Score:	Kneeling Score:	Standing Score:	**Total Score:**	

Date:	Rifle:	Scope:	Sling Used:	Notes:
Sitting Score:	Kneeling Score:	Standing Score:	**Total Score:**	

Date:	Rifle:	Scope:	Sling Used:	Notes:
Sitting Score:	Kneeling Score:	Standing Score:	**Total Score:**	

Date:	Rifle:	Scope:	Sling Used:	Notes:
Sitting Score:	Kneeling Score:	Standing Score:	**Total Score:**	

Date:	Rifle:	Scope:	Sling Used:	Notes:
Sitting Score:	Kneeling Score:	Standing Score:	**Total Score:**	

SIT, KNEEL, STAND (SLING)

Date:	Rifle:	Scope:	Sling Used:	Notes:
Sitting Score:	Kneeling Score:	Standing Score:	**Total Score:**	

Date:	Rifle:	Scope:	Sling Used:	Notes:
Sitting Score:	Kneeling Score:	Standing Score:	**Total Score:**	

Date:	Rifle:	Scope:	Sling Used:	Notes:
Sitting Score:	Kneeling Score:	Standing Score:	**Total Score:**	

Date:	Rifle:	Scope:	Sling Used:	Notes:
Sitting Score:	Kneeling Score:	Standing Score:	**Total Score:**	

Date:	Rifle:	Scope:	Sling Used:	Notes:
Sitting Score:	Kneeling Score:	Standing Score:	**Total Score:**	

Precision Rifle ©

Position Drills - 1

SIT, KNEEL, STAND (SLING)

www.GUNFIGHTERSERIES.com ©

Date:	Rifle:	Scope:	Sling Used:	Notes:
Sitting Score:	Kneeling Score:	Standing Score:	**Total Score:**	

Date:	Rifle:	Scope:	Sling Used:	Notes:
Sitting Score:	Kneeling Score:	Standing Score:	**Total Score:**	

Date:	Rifle:	Scope:	Sling Used:	Notes:
Sitting Score:	Kneeling Score:	Standing Score:	**Total Score:**	

Date:	Rifle:	Scope:	Sling Used:	Notes:
Sitting Score:	Kneeling Score:	Standing Score:	**Total Score:**	

Date:	Rifle:	Scope:	Sling Used:	Notes:
Sitting Score:	Kneeling Score:	Standing Score:	**Total Score:**	

SIT, KNEEL, STAND (SLING)

Date:	Rifle:	Scope:	Sling Used:	Notes:
Sitting Score:	Kneeling Score:	Standing Score:	**Total Score:**	

Date:	Rifle:	Scope:	Sling Used:	Notes:
Sitting Score:	Kneeling Score:	Standing Score:	**Total Score:**	

Date:	Rifle:	Scope:	Sling Used:	Notes:
Sitting Score:	Kneeling Score:	Standing Score:	**Total Score:**	

Date:	Rifle:	Scope:	Sling Used:	Notes:
Sitting Score:	Kneeling Score:	Standing Score:	**Total Score:**	

Date:	Rifle:	Scope:	Sling Used:	Notes:
Sitting Score:	Kneeling Score:	Standing Score:	**Total Score:**	

Precision Rifle ©

Position Drills - 1

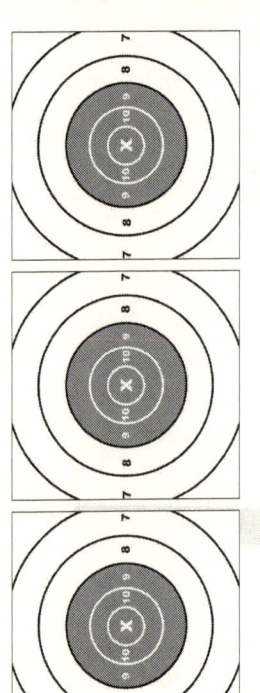

SIT, KNEEL, STAND (SUPPORTED)

Purpose: Increase proficiency and accuracy in multiple supported shooting positions.

Distance: 100 Yards.

Target: GF-2 X 3

Par Time: 2 Minutes per stage.

Extra Equipment Needed: Shot timer. Tripod or barricade shooting support.

Rounds Fired Per Stage: 3 Rounds.   **Total Rounds Fired:** 9 Rounds.

Point Penalty: As per target score.

Repetitions: 1 Rep of 3 stages.

Starting Position & Condition: See description for position. Condition 1.

Description Sitting: Assume a good sitting position utilizing a tripod or barricade support. At the timer beep, slow fire 3 rounds into the first target.

Description Kneeling: Assume a good kneeling position utilizing a tripod or barricade support. At the timer beep, slow fire 3 rounds into the second target.

Description Standing: Assume a good standing position utilizing a tripod or barricade support. At the timer beep, slow fire 3 rounds into the third target. Score targets and add all three target scores.

Goals: Novice: 80 points under par.   Expert: 90 points under par.   Gunfighter: 90 points with 9 X's under par.

Variations: Start from a standing low ready position and give yourself a 45 second par time per 3 shot repetition.

SIT, KNEEL, STAND (SUPPORTED)

Date:	Rifle:	Support Used:	Notes:
Sitting Score:	Kneeling Score:	Standing Score:	Total Score:

Date:	Rifle:	Support Used:	Notes:
Sitting Score:	Kneeling Score:	Standing Score:	Total Score:

Date:	Rifle:	Support Used:	Notes:
Sitting Score:	Kneeling Score:	Standing Score:	Total Score:

Date:	Rifle:	Support Used:	Notes:
Sitting Score:	Kneeling Score:	Standing Score:	Total Score:

Date:	Rifle:	Support Used:	Notes:
Sitting Score:	Kneeling Score:	Standing Score:	Total Score:

Precision Rifle ©

Position Drills - 2

SIT, KNEEL, STAND (SUPPORTED)

Date:	Rifle:	Support Used:	Notes:
Sitting Score:	Kneeling Score:	Standing Score:	Total Score:

Date:	Rifle:	Support Used:	Notes:
Sitting Score:	Kneeling Score:	Standing Score:	Total Score:

Date:	Rifle:	Support Used:	Notes:
Sitting Score:	Kneeling Score:	Standing Score:	Total Score:

Date:	Rifle:	Support Used:	Notes:
Sitting Score:	Kneeling Score:	Standing Score:	Total Score:

Date:	Rifle:	Support Used:	Notes:
Sitting Score:	Kneeling Score:	Standing Score:	Total Score:

www.GUNFIGHTERSERIES.com ©

SIT, KNEEL, STAND (SUPPORTED)

Date:	Rifle:	Support Used:	Notes:
Sitting Score:	Kneeling Score:	Standing Score:	Total Score:

Date:	Rifle:	Support Used:	Notes:
Sitting Score:	Kneeling Score:	Standing Score:	Total Score:

Date:	Rifle:	Support Used:	Notes:
Sitting Score:	Kneeling Score:	Standing Score:	Total Score:

Date:	Rifle:	Support Used:	Notes:
Sitting Score:	Kneeling Score:	Standing Score:	Total Score:

Date:	Rifle:	Support Used:	Notes:
Sitting Score:	Kneeling Score:	Standing Score:	Total Score:

Precision Rifle ©

Position Drills - 2

www.GUNFIGHTERSERIES.com ©

SIT, KNEEL, STAND (SUPPORTED)

Date:	Rifle:	Support Used:	Notes:
Sitting Score:	Kneeling Score:	Standing Score:	Total Score:

Date:	Rifle:	Support Used:	Notes:
Sitting Score:	Kneeling Score:	Standing Score:	Total Score:

Date:	Rifle:	Support Used:	Notes:
Sitting Score:	Kneeling Score:	Standing Score:	Total Score:

Date:	Rifle:	Support Used:	Notes:
Sitting Score:	Kneeling Score:	Standing Score:	Total Score:

Date:	Rifle:	Support Used:	Notes:
Sitting Score:	Kneeling Score:	Standing Score:	Total Score:

SIT, KNEEL, STAND (SUPPORTED)

Date:	Rifle:	Support Used:	Notes:
Sitting Score:	Kneeling Score:	Standing Score:	Total Score:

Date:	Rifle:	Support Used:	Notes:
Sitting Score:	Kneeling Score:	Standing Score:	Total Score:

Date:	Rifle:	Support Used:	Notes:
Sitting Score:	Kneeling Score:	Standing Score:	Total Score:

Date:	Rifle:	Support Used:	Notes:
Sitting Score:	Kneeling Score:	Standing Score:	Total Score:

Date:	Rifle:	Support Used:	Notes:
Sitting Score:	Kneeling Score:	Standing Score:	Total Score:

Precision Rifle ©

Position Drills - 2

DOT TORTURE

Purpose: To learn and test your accuracy limits.

Distance: 100 Yards.

Target: KYRL

Rounds Fired Per String: 5 Rounds.

Total Rounds Fired: 15 Rounds.

Point Penalty: Per target score.

Repetitions: 1 Rep of 3 strings.

Starting Position & Condition: See string description. Condition 1.

Description:

String 1: On your personal go from a good prone shooting position, either supported or with sling, fire 1 round into each dot on the far left column starting from the biggest on top to the smallest on bottom. Log your accuracy dot size limit.

String 2: On your personal go from a kneeling shooting position, either supported or with sling, fire 1 round into each dot in the middle column starting at the biggest on top to the smallest dot. Log your accuracy dot size limit.

String 2: On your personal go from a standing shooting position, either supported or with sling, fire 1 round into each dot in the far right column starting at the biggest on top to the smallest dot. Log your accuracy dot size limit.

Goals: Novice: 18 Points   Expert: 30 Points   Gunfighter: 45 Points

Variations:

⊕ Give yourself a par time of 45 seconds per string.

⊕ Start 10 yards behind firing position.

DOT TORTURE

Date:			Location:					Rifle:	Scope:	Ammo:
Rep 1 Dots:	.5" /	.75" /	1" /	1.5" /	2"			Rep 1 Score:		Supported / Unsupported / Sling
Rep 2 Dots:	.5" /	.75" /	1" /	1.5" /	2"			Rep 2 Score:		Support Type:
Rep 3 Dots:	.5" /	.75" /	1" /	1.5" /	2"			Rep 3 Score:		**Total Score:**
Notes:										

Date:			Location:					Rifle:	Scope:	Ammo:
Rep 1 Dots:	.5" /	.75" /	1" /	1.5" /	2"			Rep 1 Score:		Supported / Unsupported / Sling
Rep 2 Dots:	.5" /	.75" /	1" /	1.5" /	2"			Rep 2 Score:		Support Type:
Rep 3 Dots:	.5" /	.75" /	1" /	1.5" /	2"			Rep 3 Score:		**Total Score:**
Notes:										

Date:			Location:					Rifle:	Scope:	Ammo:
Rep 1 Dots:	.5" /	.75" /	1" /	1.5" /	2"			Rep 1 Score:		Supported / Unsupported / Sling
Rep 2 Dots:	.5" /	.75" /	1" /	1.5" /	2"			Rep 2 Score:		Support Type:
Rep 3 Dots:	.5" /	.75" /	1" /	1.5" /	2"			Rep 3 Score:		**Total Score:**
Notes:										

Precision Rifle ©

Position Drills - 3

DOT TORTURE

www.GUNFIGHTERSERIES.com ©

Date:			Location:							Rifle:		Scope:	Ammo:
Rep 1 Dots:	.5"	/	.75"	/	1"	/	1.5"	/	2"	Rep 1 Score:			Supported / Unsupported / Sling
Rep 2 Dots:	.5"	/	.75"	/	1"	/	1.5"	/	2"	Rep 2 Score:			Support Type:
Rep 3 Dots:	.5"	/	.75"	/	1"	/	1.5"	/	2"	Rep 3 Score:			**Total Score:**
Notes:													

Date:			Location:							Rifle:		Scope:	Ammo:
Rep 1 Dots:	.5"	/	.75"	/	1"	/	1.5"	/	2"	Rep 1 Score:			Supported / Unsupported / Sling
Rep 2 Dots:	.5"	/	.75"	/	1"	/	1.5"	/	2"	Rep 2 Score:			Support Type:
Rep 3 Dots:	.5"	/	.75"	/	1"	/	1.5"	/	2"	Rep 3 Score:			**Total Score:**
Notes:													

Date:			Location:							Rifle:		Scope:	Ammo:
Rep 1 Dots:	.5"	/	.75"	/	1"	/	1.5"	/	2"	Rep 1 Score:			Supported / Unsupported / Sling
Rep 2 Dots:	.5"	/	.75"	/	1"	/	1.5"	/	2"	Rep 2 Score:			Support Type:
Rep 3 Dots:	.5"	/	.75"	/	1"	/	1.5"	/	2"	Rep 3 Score:			**Total Score:**
Notes:													

DOT TORTURE

Date:			Location:					Rifle:	Scope:	Ammo:
Rep 1 Dots:	.5"	/ .75"	/	1"	/ 1.5"	/	2"	Rep 1 Score:		Supported / Unsupported / Sling
Rep 2 Dots:	.5"	/ .75"	/	1"	/ 1.5"	/	2"	Rep 2 Score:		Support Type:
Rep 3 Dots:	.5"	/ .75"	/	1"	/ 1.5"	/	2"	Rep 3 Score:		**Total Score:**
Notes:										

Date:			Location:					Rifle:	Scope:	Ammo:
Rep 1 Dots:	.5"	/ .75"	/	1"	/ 1.5"	/	2"	Rep 1 Score:		Supported / Unsupported / Sling
Rep 2 Dots:	.5"	/ .75"	/	1"	/ 1.5"	/	2"	Rep 2 Score:		Support Type:
Rep 3 Dots:	.5"	/ .75"	/	1"	/ 1.5"	/	2"	Rep 3 Score:		**Total Score:**
Notes:										

Date:			Location:					Rifle:	Scope:	Ammo:
Rep 1 Dots:	.5"	/ .75"	/	1"	/ 1.5"	/	2"	Rep 1 Score:		Supported / Unsupported / Sling
Rep 2 Dots:	.5"	/ .75"	/	1"	/ 1.5"	/	2"	Rep 2 Score:		Support Type:
Rep 3 Dots:	.5"	/ .75"	/	1"	/ 1.5"	/	2"	Rep 3 Score:		**Total Score:**
Notes:										

DOT TORTURE

Date:			Location:			
Rep 1 Dots:	.5" /	.75" /	1" /	1.5" /	2"	
Rep 2 Dots:	.5" /	.75" /	1" /	1.5" /	2"	
Rep 3 Dots:	.5" /	.75" /	1" /	1.5" /	2"	
Notes:						

Rifle:		Scope:		Ammo:	
Rep 1 Score:				Supported / Unsupported / Sling	
Rep 2 Score:				Support Type:	
Rep 3 Score:				**Total Score:**	

Date:			Location:			
Rep 1 Dots:	.5" /	.75" /	1" /	1.5" /	2"	
Rep 2 Dots:	.5" /	.75" /	1" /	1.5" /	2"	
Rep 3 Dots:	.5" /	.75" /	1" /	1.5" /	2"	
Notes:						

Rifle:		Scope:		Ammo:	
Rep 1 Score:				Supported / Unsupported / Sling	
Rep 2 Score:				Support Type:	
Rep 3 Score:				**Total Score:**	

Date:			Location:			
Rep 1 Dots:	.5" /	.75" /	1" /	1.5" /	2"	
Rep 2 Dots:	.5" /	.75" /	1" /	1.5" /	2"	
Rep 3 Dots:	.5" /	.75" /	1" /	1.5" /	2"	
Notes:						

Rifle:		Scope:		Ammo:	
Rep 1 Score:				Supported / Unsupported / Sling	
Rep 2 Score:				Support Type:	
Rep 3 Score:				**Total Score:**	

www.GUNFIGHTERSERIES.com ©

DOT TORTURE

○ ○ ○ ○ ○ ○ ○ ○ ○ ○ ○ ○ ○ ○ ○
○ ○ ○ ○ ○ ○ ○ ○ ○ ○ ○ ○ ○ ○ ○
○ ○ ○ ○ ○ ○ ○ ○ ○ ○ ○ ○ ○ ○ ○

Date:		Location:				Rifle:	Scope:	Ammo:
Rep 1 Dots:	.5" / .75" /	1" /	1.5" /	2"		Rep 1 Score:		Supported / Unsupported / Sling
Rep 2 Dots:	.5" / .75" /	1" /	1.5" /	2"		Rep 2 Score:		Support Type:
Rep 3 Dots:	.5" / .75" /	1" /	1.5" /	2"		Rep 3 Score:		**Total Score:**
Notes:								

Date:		Location:				Rifle:	Scope:	Ammo:
Rep 1 Dots:	.5" / .75" /	1" /	1.5" /	2"		Rep 1 Score:		Supported / Unsupported / Sling
Rep 2 Dots:	.5" / .75" /	1" /	1.5" /	2"		Rep 2 Score:		Support Type:
Rep 3 Dots:	.5" / .75" /	1" /	1.5" /	2"		Rep 3 Score:		**Total Score:**
Notes:								

Date:		Location:				Rifle:	Scope:	Ammo:
Rep 1 Dots:	.5" / .75" /	1" /	1.5" /	2"		Rep 1 Score:		Supported / Unsupported / Sling
Rep 2 Dots:	.5" / .75" /	1" /	1.5" /	2"		Rep 2 Score:		Support Type:
Rep 3 Dots:	.5" / .75" /	1" /	1.5" /	2"		Rep 3 Score:		**Total Score:**
Notes:								

Precision Rifle ©

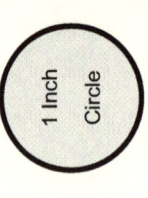

1 Inch Circle

PRONE VS. POSITIONAL

Purpose: To reinforce natural point of aim and increase accuracy with pone and positional positions.

By: Francis Colon

Distance: 100 Yards.

Par Time: Per goal standard.

Target: 1 Inch circles.

Extra Equipment Needed: Shot timer. A medium to high barricade for support.

Rounds Fired Per Rep: 5 Rounds.

Total Rounds Fired: 10 Rounds.

Point Penalty: 1 Point for in or touching the circle. Minus 1 point for outside the circle.

Repetitions: 2 Reps.

Starting Position & Condition: Standing - Low ready. Condition 1.

Description:

Repetition 1: At the timer beep, assume a good prone supported position and 5 rounds into a 1 inch circle. Record your score.

Repetition 2: At the timer beep, assume a good kneeling or standing supported position and 5 rounds into a 1 inch circle. Record your score.

Goals: Novice: 8 Point under 75 seconds. **Expert:** 10 Point under 60 seconds. **Gunfighter:** 10 Point under 45 seconds.

Variations: Shoot this same drill on 1 MOA paper or steel targets at 200, 300 and 400 yards.

www.GUNFIGHTERSERIES.com ©

PRONE VS. POSITIONAL

Prone   Positional

○ ○ ○ ○ ○
○ ○ ○ ○ ○

Date:	Rifle	Scope:	Ammo:
Prone Time:	Prone Score:	Positional Time:	Positional Score:
Total Score:	Barricade Type:	Notes:	
Date:	Rifle	Scope:	Ammo:
Prone Time:	Prone Score:	Positional Time:	Positional Score:
Total Score:	Barricade Type:	Notes:	
Date:	Rifle	Scope:	Ammo:
Prone Time:	Prone Score:	Positional Time:	Positional Score:
Total Score:	Barricade Type:	Notes:	
Date:	Rifle	Scope:	Ammo:
Prone Time:	Prone Score:	Positional Time:	Positional Score:
Total Score:	Barricade Type:	Notes:	
Date:	Rifle	Scope:	Ammo:
Prone Time:	Prone Score:	Positional Time:	Positional Score:
Total Score:	Barricade Type:	Notes:	

PRONE VS. POSITIONAL

Date:	Rifle	Scope:	Ammo:
Prone Time:	Prone Score:	Positional Time:	Positional Score:
Total Score:	Barricade Type:	Notes:	
Date:	Rifle	Scope:	Ammo:
Prone Time:	Prone Score:	Positional Time:	Positional Score:
Total Score:	Barricade Type:	Notes:	
Date:	Rifle	Scope:	Ammo:
Prone Time:	Prone Score:	Positional Time:	Positional Score:
Total Score:	Barricade Type:	Notes:	
Date:	Rifle	Scope:	Ammo:
Prone Time:	Prone Score:	Positional Time:	Positional Score:
Total Score:	Barricade Type:	Notes:	
Date:	Rifle	Scope:	Ammo:
Prone Time:	Prone Score:	Positional Time:	Positional Score:
Total Score:	Barricade Type:	Notes:	

PRONE VS. POSITIONAL

Prone   Positional

○ ○ ○ ○ ○
○ ○ ○ ○ ○

Date:	Rifle	Scope:	Ammo:
Prone Time:	Prone Score:	Positional Time:	Positional Score:
Total Score:	Barricade Type:	Notes:	
Date:	Rifle	Scope:	Ammo:
Prone Time:	Prone Score:	Positional Time:	Positional Score:
Total Score:	Barricade Type:	Notes:	
Date:	Rifle	Scope:	Ammo:
Prone Time:	Prone Score:	Positional Time:	Positional Score:
Total Score:	Barricade Type:	Notes:	
Date:	Rifle	Scope:	Ammo:
Prone Time:	Prone Score:	Positional Time:	Positional Score:
Total Score:	Barricade Type:	Notes:	
Date:	Rifle	Scope:	Ammo:
Prone Time:	Prone Score:	Positional Time:	Positional Score:
Total Score:	Barricade Type:	Notes:	

Precision Rifle ©

PRONE VS. POSITIONAL

Prone   Positional

Date:	Rifle	Scope:	Ammo:
Prone Time:	Prone Score:	Positional Time:	Positional Score:
Total Score:	Barricade Type:	Notes:	
Date:	Rifle	Scope:	Ammo:
Prone Time:	Prone Score:	Positional Time:	Positional Score:
Total Score:	Barricade Type:	Notes:	
Date:	Rifle	Scope:	Ammo:
Prone Time:	Prone Score:	Positional Time:	Positional Score:
Total Score:	Barricade Type:	Notes:	
Date:	Rifle	Scope:	Ammo:
Prone Time:	Prone Score:	Positional Time:	Positional Score:
Total Score:	Barricade Type:	Notes:	
Date:	Rifle	Scope:	Ammo:
Prone Time:	Prone Score:	Positional Time:	Positional Score:
Total Score:	Barricade Type:	Notes:	

www.GUNFIGHTERSERIES.com ©

PRONE VS. POSITIONAL

Prone | Positional

Date:	Rifle	Scope:	Ammo:
Prone Time:	Prone Score:	Positional Time:	Positional Score:
Total Score:	Barricade Type:	Notes:	
Date:	Rifle	Scope:	Ammo:
Prone Time:	Prone Score:	Positional Time:	Positional Score:
Total Score:	Barricade Type:	Notes:	
Date:	Rifle	Scope:	Ammo:
Prone Time:	Prone Score:	Positional Time:	Positional Score:
Total Score:	Barricade Type:	Notes:	
Date:	Rifle	Scope:	Ammo:
Prone Time:	Prone Score:	Positional Time:	Positional Score:
Total Score:	Barricade Type:	Notes:	
Date:	Rifle	Scope:	Ammo:
Prone Time:	Prone Score:	Positional Time:	Positional Score:
Total Score:	Barricade Type:	Notes:	

Precision Rifle ©

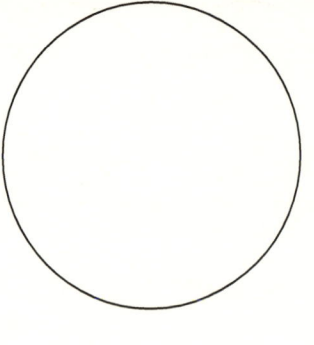

THREESOME

Purpose: Increase position transition speed and accuracy.

By: Francis Colon

Distance: 400 Yards.

Target: Per goal standard. (20, 14 or 10 inch steel circle.)

Par Time: 90 Seconds max. See goal standards.

Extra Equipment Needed: Shot timer. A barricade with at least 4 different kneeling or standing support positions.

Total Rounds Fired: 8 Rounds.

Point Penalty: Time plus penalty.

Repetitions: 1 Rep.

Starting Position & Condition: Standing - Low Ready starting 10 feet behind barricade. Condition 4.

Description: Record atmospherics and elevation/wind adjustments for range to target. At the timer beep, move to the barricade's 1st supported position, load and make ready your rifle, and engage the steel circle target with 2 rounds. Then move to the 2nd support position and engage the same steel circle target with 2 rounds. Continue at the 3rd and 4th support positions. Record your time, score and penalty. Add 5 seconds for each miss.

Goals: Novice: 60 Second using a 20" target.   Expert: 50 Seconds using a 14" target.   Gunfighter: 45 Seconds using a 10" target.

Variations:

⊕ Dry Fire 1 rep for pure speed on a 20" target. Dry fire 1 rep for pure precision on a 4-6" target. Live fire 1 rep for score on a 10" target.

THREESOME

○ ○ ○ ○ ○

Date:	Rifle:	Scope:	Dial Elev / Reticle Hold Over
Temp:	Humidity:	Baro:	Elevation Adj:
Target Size:	Barricade Type:		Notes:
Time:	Penalty:	Total Time Score:	
Date:	Rifle:	Scope:	Dial Elev / Reticle Hold Over
Temp:	Humidity:	Baro:	Elevation Adj:
Target Size:	Barricade Type:		Notes:
Time:	Penalty:	Total Time Score:	
Date:	Rifle:	Scope:	Dial Elev / Reticle Hold Over
Temp:	Humidity:	Baro:	Elevation Adj:
Target Size:	Barricade Type:		Notes:
Time:	Penalty:	Total Time Score:	
Date:	Rifle:	Scope:	Dial Elev / Reticle Hold Over
Temp:	Humidity:	Baro:	Elevation Adj:
Target Size:	Barricade Type:		Notes:
Time:	Penalty:	Total Time Score:	
Date:	Rifle:	Scope:	Dial Elev / Reticle Hold Over
Temp:	Humidity:	Baro:	Elevation Adj:
Target Size:	Barricade Type:		Notes:
Time:	Penalty:	Total Time Score:	

Position Drills - 5

Precision Rifle ©

THREESOME

Date:	Rifle:	Scope:		Dial Elev / Reticle Hold Over
Temp:	Humidity:	Baro:		Elevation Adj:
Target Size:	Barricade Type:			Notes:
Time:	Penalty:	Total Time Score:		
Date:	Rifle:	Scope:		Dial Elev / Reticle Hold Over
Temp:	Humidity:	Baro:		Elevation Adj:
Target Size:	Barricade Type:			Notes:
Time:	Penalty:	Total Time Score:		
Date:	Rifle:	Scope:		Dial Elev / Reticle Hold Over
Temp:	Humidity:	Baro:		Elevation Adj:
Target Size:	Barricade Type:			Notes:
Time:	Penalty:	Total Time Score:		
Date:	Rifle:	Scope:		Dial Elev / Reticle Hold Over
Temp:	Humidity:	Baro:		Elevation Adj:
Target Size:	Barricade Type:			Notes:
Time:	Penalty:	Total Time Score:		
Date:	Rifle:	Scope:		Dial Elev / Reticle Hold Over
Temp:	Humidity:	Baro:		Elevation Adj:
Target Size:	Barricade Type:			Notes:
Time:	Penalty:	Total Time Score:		

www.GUNFIGHTERSERIES.com ©

THREESOME

Date:	Rifle:	Scope:	Dial Elev / Reticle Hold Over
Temp:	Humidity:	Baro:	Elevation Adj:
Target Size:	Barricade Type:		Notes:
Time:	Penalty:	Total Time Score:	
Date:	Rifle:	Scope:	Dial Elev / Reticle Hold Over
Temp:	Humidity:	Baro:	Elevation Adj:
Target Size:	Barricade Type:		Notes:
Time:	Penalty:	Total Time Score:	
Date:	Rifle:	Scope:	Dial Elev / Reticle Hold Over
Temp:	Humidity:	Baro:	Elevation Adj:
Target Size:	Barricade Type:		Notes:
Time:	Penalty:	Total Time Score:	
Date:	Rifle:	Scope:	Dial Elev / Reticle Hold Over
Temp:	Humidity:	Baro:	Elevation Adj:
Target Size:	Barricade Type:		Notes:
Time:	Penalty:	Total Time Score:	
Date:	Rifle:	Scope:	Dial Elev / Reticle Hold Over
Temp:	Humidity:	Baro:	Elevation Adj:
Target Size:	Barricade Type:		Notes:
Time:	Penalty:	Total Time Score:	

THREESOME

Date:	Rifle:	Scope:	Dial Elev / Reticle Hold Over
Temp:	Humidity:	Baro:	Elevation Adj:
Target Size:	Barricade Type:		Notes:
Time:	Penalty:	Total Time Score:	
Date:	Rifle:	Scope:	Dial Elev / Reticle Hold Over
Temp:	Humidity:	Baro:	Elevation Adj:
Target Size:	Barricade Type:		Notes:
Time:	Penalty:	Total Time Score:	
Date:	Rifle:	Scope:	Dial Elev / Reticle Hold Over
Temp:	Humidity:	Baro:	Elevation Adj:
Target Size:	Barricade Type:		Notes:
Time:	Penalty:	Total Time Score:	
Date:	Rifle:	Scope:	Dial Elev / Reticle Hold Over
Temp:	Humidity:	Baro:	Elevation Adj:
Target Size:	Barricade Type:		Notes:
Time:	Penalty:	Total Time Score:	
Date:	Rifle:	Scope:	Dial Elev / Reticle Hold Over
Temp:	Humidity:	Baro:	Elevation Adj:
Target Size:	Barricade Type:		Notes:
Time:	Penalty:	Total Time Score:	

THREESOME

Date:	Rifle:	Scope:	Dial Elev / Reticle Hold Over
Temp:	Humidity:	Baro:	Elevation Adj:
Target Size:	Barricade Type:		Notes:
Time:	Penalty:	Total Time Score:	

Date:	Rifle:	Scope:	Dial Elev / Reticle Hold Over
Temp:	Humidity:	Baro:	Elevation Adj:
Target Size:	Barricade Type:		Notes:
Time:	Penalty:	Total Time Score:	

Date:	Rifle:	Scope:	Dial Elev / Reticle Hold Over
Temp:	Humidity:	Baro:	Elevation Adj:
Target Size:	Barricade Type:		Notes:
Time:	Penalty:	Total Time Score:	

Date:	Rifle:	Scope:	Dial Elev / Reticle Hold Over
Temp:	Humidity:	Baro:	Elevation Adj:
Target Size:	Barricade Type:		Notes:
Time:	Penalty:	Total Time Score:	

Date:	Rifle:	Scope:	Dial Elev / Reticle Hold Over
Temp:	Humidity:	Baro:	Elevation Adj:
Target Size:	Barricade Type:		Notes:
Time:	Penalty:	Total Time Score:	

SNIPER DICE

Purpose: Increase proficiency and accuracy in various shooting positions.

Distance: 200 - 750 Yards. (Increase distance with proficiency)

Target: Target: Steel silhouettes X 6.

Par Time: 30 Seconds per shot.

Extra Equipment Needed: Shot timer. High, medium and low barricade. 2 Dice. Shooting partner with spotting scope.

Rounds Fired Per Rep: 1 Round.   **Total Rounds Fired:** 15 Rounds.

Point Penalty: Hit / Miss.

Starting Position & Condition: Standing. Rifle placed on the firing line set at personal ZERO. Condition 4.

Set Up: Write down on the data sheet the description and distance of any 6 targets at varying ranges from 200 - 750 yards. (Closer ranges for novice shooters). You may also fill in your elevation / wind adjustments at this time for each target. Next write down 6 different shooting positions which may be supported or unsupported. Example: Standing with a barrel barricade, kneeling with sling only, prone bipod supported, etc.

Description: At the timer beep, roll the dice. The number on the BLACK DIE indicates the target to engage. The number on the WHITE DIE indicates the shooting position to use. Load your rifle with 1 round, assume a good shooting position and engage your prescribed target with one round. Record shot time and hit location then return the rifle to the shooting line in condition 4. Repeat for a total of 15 shots, rolling the dice for each engagement.

Goals: Novice: 10 Hits under par.   Expert: 15 Hits under par.   Gunfighter: 15 Hits under 45 sec par using the below variation.

Variation: Begin the drill by writing down the target description but not the distance. When you roll the dice, you must range the target and calculate elevation and windage while on the clock.

SNIPER DICE

Date:	Location:	Rifle:	Scope:
Ammo:	MV:	Temp:	Baro:

Target ID:	Dist:	Elev:	10 MPH Wind:	
Target ID:	Dist:	Elev:	10 MPH Wind:	
Target ID:	Dist:	Elev:	10 MPH Wind:	
Target ID:	Dist:	Elev:	10 MPH Wind:	
Target ID:	Dist:	Elev:	10 MPH Wind:	
Target ID:	Dist:	Elev:	10 MPH Wind:	

BLACK

Shooting Position	Supported	Support Type
	Yes / No	
	Yes / No	
	Yes / No	
	Yes / No	
	Yes / No	
	Yes / No	

WHITE

SCORING

Shot	Shot Time	Score
1	Sec.	Hit / Miss
2	Sec.	Hit / Miss
3	Sec.	Hit / Miss
4	Sec.	Hit / Miss
5	Sec.	Hit / Miss
6	Sec.	Hit / Miss
7	Sec.	Hit / Miss
8	Sec.	Hit / Miss
9	Sec.	Hit / Miss
10	Sec.	Hit / Miss
11	Sec.	Hit / Miss
12	Sec.	Hit / Miss
13	Sec.	Hit / Miss
14	Sec.	Hit / Miss
15	Sec.	Hit / Miss
Total Score:		

Position Drills - 6

Precision Rifle ©

SNIPER DICE

Date:		Location:		Rifle:		Scope:	
Ammo:		MV:		Temp:		Baro:	
Target ID:		Dist:		Elev:		10 MPH Wind:	
Target ID:		Dist:		Elev:		10 MPH Wind:	
Target ID:		Dist:		Elev:		10 MPH Wind:	
Target ID:		Dist:		Elev:		10 MPH Wind:	
Target ID:		Dist:		Elev:		10 MPH Wind:	
Target ID:		Dist:		Elev:		10 MPH Wind:	
Shooting Position		Supported	Support Type				
		Yes / No					
		Yes / No					
		Yes / No					
		Yes / No					
		Yes / No					

BLACK ⚀ ⚁ ⚂ ⚃ ⚄ ⚅
WHITE ⚀ ⚁ ⚂ ⚃ ⚄ ⚅

SCORING

Shot	Shot Time	Score
1	Sec.	Hit / Miss
2	Sec.	Hit / Miss
3	Sec.	Hit / Miss
4	Sec.	Hit / Miss
5	Sec.	Hit / Miss
6	Sec.	Hit / Miss
7	Sec.	Hit / Miss
8	Sec.	Hit / Miss
9	Sec.	Hit / Miss
10	Sec.	Hit / Miss
11	Sec.	Hit / Miss
12	Sec.	Hit / Miss
13	Sec.	Hit / Miss
14	Sec.	Hit / Miss
15	Sec.	Hit / Miss
Total Score:		

SNIPER DICE

Date:	Location:	Rifle:	Scope:
Ammo:	MV:	Temp:	Baro:

	Target ID:	Dist:	Elev:	10 MPH Wind:
BLACK	Target ID:	Dist:	Elev:	10 MPH Wind:
	Target ID:	Dist:	Elev:	10 MPH Wind:
	Target ID:	Dist:	Elev:	10 MPH Wind:
	Target ID:	Dist:	Elev:	10 MPH Wind:
	Target ID:	Dist:	Elev:	10 MPH Wind:

Shooting Position	Supported	Support Type
	Yes / No	
WHITE	Yes / No	
	Yes / No	
	Yes / No	
	Yes / No	
	Yes / No	

SCORING

Shot	Shot Time	Score
1	Sec.	Hit / Miss
2	Sec.	Hit / Miss
3	Sec.	Hit / Miss
4	Sec.	Hit / Miss
5	Sec.	Hit / Miss
6	Sec.	Hit / Miss
7	Sec.	Hit / Miss
8	Sec.	Hit / Miss
9	Sec.	Hit / Miss
10	Sec.	Hit / Miss
11	Sec.	Hit / Miss
12	Sec.	Hit / Miss
13	Sec.	Hit / Miss
14	Sec.	Hit / Miss
15	Sec.	Hit / Miss
Total Score:		

Position Drills - 6

Precision Rifle ©

SNIPER DICE

www.GUNFIGHTERSERIES.com ©

Date:	Location:	Rifle:	Scope:
Ammo:	MV:	Temp:	Baro:

Target ID:	Dist:	Elev:	10 MPH Wind:
Target ID:	Dist:	Elev:	10 MPH Wind:
Target ID:	Dist:	Elev:	10 MPH Wind:
Target ID:	Dist:	Elev:	10 MPH Wind:
Target ID:	Dist:	Elev:	10 MPH Wind:
Target ID:	Dist:	Elev:	10 MPH Wind:

Shooting Position	Supported	Support Type
	Yes / No	
	Yes / No	
	Yes / No	
	Yes / No	
	Yes / No	
	Yes / No	

BLACK ⚀ ⚁ ⚂ ⚃ ⚄ ⚅

WHITE ⚀ ⚁ ⚂ ⚃ ⚄ ⚅

SCORING

Shot	Shot Time	Score
1	Sec.	Hit / Miss
2	Sec.	Hit / Miss
3	Sec.	Hit / Miss
4	Sec.	Hit / Miss
5	Sec.	Hit / Miss
6	Sec.	Hit / Miss
7	Sec.	Hit / Miss
8	Sec.	Hit / Miss
9	Sec.	Hit / Miss
10	Sec.	Hit / Miss
11	Sec.	Hit / Miss
12	Sec.	Hit / Miss
13	Sec.	Hit / Miss
14	Sec.	Hit / Miss
15	Sec.	Hit / Miss
Total Score:		

SNIPER DICE

Date:	Location:	Rifle:	Scope:
Ammo:	MV:	Temp:	Baro:

	Target ID:	Dist:	Elev:	10 MPH Wind:
BLACK	Target ID:	Dist:	Elev:	10 MPH Wind:
	Target ID:	Dist:	Elev:	10 MPH Wind:
	Target ID:	Dist:	Elev:	10 MPH Wind:
	Target ID:	Dist:	Elev:	10 MPH Wind:
	Target ID:	Dist:	Elev:	10 MPH Wind:

Shooting Position	Supported	Support Type
	Yes / No	
WHITE	Yes / No	
	Yes / No	
	Yes / No	
	Yes / No	
	Yes / No	

SCORING

Shot	Shot Time	Score
1	Sec.	Hit / Miss
2	Sec.	Hit / Miss
3	Sec.	Hit / Miss
4	Sec.	Hit / Miss
5	Sec.	Hit / Miss
6	Sec.	Hit / Miss
7	Sec.	Hit / Miss
8	Sec.	Hit / Miss
9	Sec.	Hit / Miss
10	Sec.	Hit / Miss
11	Sec.	Hit / Miss
12	Sec.	Hit / Miss
13	Sec.	Hit / Miss
14	Sec.	Hit / Miss
15	Sec.	Hit / Miss
Total Score:		

Position Drills - 6

Precision Rifle ©

LATERAL SHUFFLE

Purpose: To gauge proficiency and accuracy in tracking lateral targets.

Distance: 25 Yards.

Target: GF-2 X 3 (at least 50ft apart, further apart the better)

Par Time: 30 Seconds per stage.

Extra Equipment Needed: Shot timer.

Rounds Fired Per Stage: 3 Rounds.   **Total Rounds Fired:** 9 Rounds.

Point Penalty: As per target score.

Starting Position & Condition: Standing low ready. Condition 1.

Description: Begin each rep in the standing low ready. At the timer beep, assume a good prone position and engage each target with 1 round each. Put rifle on safe and record your time and score. At the timer beep, assume a good kneeling position and engage each target with 1 round each. Put rifle on safe and record your time and score. At the timer beep, assume a good standing position and engage each target with 1 round each.

Note: Shift your entire body's Natural Point of Aim as you transition from one target to another.

Goals: Novice: 80 Points under par.   Expert: 90 Points under par.   Gunfighter: 90 Points with 9X's.

Variations: Decrease the par time once you achieve the Gunfighter goal.

LATERAL SHUFFLE

Prone   Kneeling   Standing

Date:	Rifle:	Scope Power:	Notes:
Prone Time:	Kneeling Time:	Standing Time:	
Prone Score:	Kneeling Score:	Standing Score:	**Total Score:**

Date:	Rifle:	Scope Power:	Notes:
Prone Time:	Kneeling Time:	Standing Time:	
Total Drill Time:	+ Penalties:	**Total Score:**	**Total Score:**

Date:	Rifle:	Scope Power:	Notes:
Prone Time:	Kneeling Time:	Standing Time:	
Total Drill Time:	+ Penalties:	**Total Score:**	**Total Score:**

Date:	Rifle:	Scope Power:	Notes:
Prone Time:	Kneeling Time:	Standing Time:	
Total Drill Time:	+ Penalties:	**Total Score:**	**Total Score:**

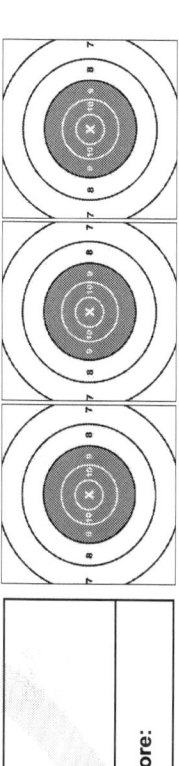

Precision Rifle ©

Multi Target Drills - 1

LATERAL SHUFFLE

www.GUNFIGHTERSERIES.com ©

Prone — Kneeling — Standing

Date:	Rifle:	Scope Power:	Notes:
Prone Time:	Kneeling Time:	Standing Time:	
Prone Score:	Kneeling Score:	Standing Score:	**Total Score:**

Date:	Rifle:	Scope Power:	Notes:
Prone Time:	Kneeling Time:	Standing Time:	
Total Drill Time:	+ Penalties:	**Total Score:**	

Date:	Rifle:	Scope Power:	Notes:
Prone Time:	Kneeling Time:	Standing Time:	
Total Drill Time:	+ Penalties:	**Total Score:**	

Date:	Rifle:	Scope Power:	Notes:
Prone Time:	Kneeling Time:	Standing Time:	
Total Drill Time:	+ Penalties:	**Total Score:**	

LATERAL SHUFFLE

Prone   Kneeling   Standing

Date:	Rifle:	Scope Power:	Notes:
Prone Time:	Kneeling Time:	Standing Time:	
Prone Score:	Kneeling Score:	Standing Score:	
Total Drill Time:	+ Penalties:	**Total Score:**	**Total Score:**

Date:	Rifle:	Scope Power:	Notes:
Prone Time:	Kneeling Time:	Standing Time:	
Prone Score:	Kneeling Score:	Standing Score:	
Total Drill Time:	+ Penalties:	**Total Score:**	**Total Score:**

Date:	Rifle:	Scope Power:	Notes:
Prone Time:	Kneeling Time:	Standing Time:	
Prone Score:	Kneeling Score:	Standing Score:	
Total Drill Time:	+ Penalties:	**Total Score:**	**Total Score:**

Date:	Rifle:	Scope Power:	Notes:
Prone Time:	Kneeling Time:	Standing Time:	
Prone Score:	Kneeling Score:	Standing Score:	
Total Drill Time:	+ Penalties:	**Total Score:**	**Total Score:**

Multi Target Drills - 1

Precision Rifle ©

LATERAL SHUFFLE

www.GUNFIGHTERSERIES.com ©

	Prone	Kneeling	Standing

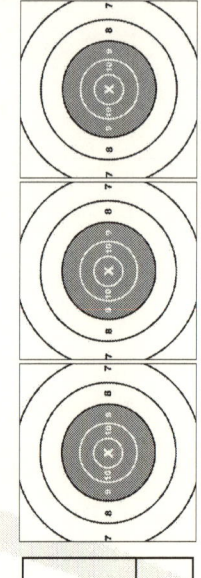

Date:	Rifle:	Scope Power:	Notes:
Prone Time:	Kneeling Time:	Standing Time:	
Prone Score:		Standing Score:	
Total Drill Time:	+ Penalties:	**Total Score:**	

Date:	Rifle:	Scope Power:	Notes:
Prone Time:	Kneeling Time:	Standing Time:	
Total Drill Time:	+ Penalties:	**Total Score:**	

Date:	Rifle:	Scope Power:	Notes:
Prone Time:	Kneeling Time:	Standing Time:	
Total Drill Time:	+ Penalties:	**Total Score:**	

Date:	Rifle:	Scope Power:	Notes:
Prone Time:	Kneeling Time:	Standing Time:	
Total Drill Time:	+ Penalties:	**Total Score:**	

LATERAL SHUFFLE

Prone — Kneeling — Standing

Date:	Rifle:	Scope Power:	Notes:
Prone Time:	Kneeling Time:	Standing Time:	
Prone Score:	Kneeling Score:	Standing Score:	
Total Drill Time:	+ Penalties:	**Total Score:**	

Date:	Rifle:	Scope Power:	Notes:
Prone Time:	Kneeling Time:	Standing Time:	
Total Drill Time:	+ Penalties:	**Total Score:**	

Date:	Rifle:	Scope Power:	Notes:
Prone Time:	Kneeling Time:	Standing Time:	
Total Drill Time:	+ Penalties:	**Total Score:**	

Date:	Rifle:	Scope Power:	Notes:
Prone Time:	Kneeling Time:	Standing Time:	
Total Drill Time:	+ Penalties:	**Total Score:**	

Precision Rifle ©

Multi Target Drills - 1

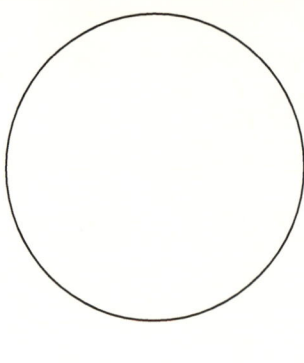
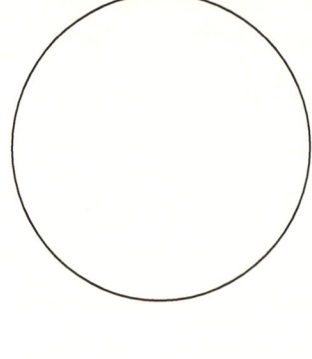

HEAD STRONG

Purpose: Increase target transition speed.

Distance: Approx. 200, 225, 250, 275, 300 Yards. (The more lateral dispersion the better).

Target: Steel circle, or head silhouette, targets no larger than 8 inches.

Extra Equipment Needed: Shot timer.

Total Rounds Fired: 6 - 10 Rounds.

Repetitions: 1 Rep.

Starting Position & Condition: Standing - Low Ready. Condition 1.

Description: Record atmospherics and elevation/wind adjustments for range to target(s). At the timer beep, assume a good prone supported position and engage the closest target. If you miss, reengage. If you score a hit, move to the next furthest target. Continue until all 5 targets have been hit, you run out of ammo, or exceed par time. All 5 targets must be hit to pass this drill.

Goals: Novice: 90 Seconds   Expert: 60 Seconds.   Gunfighter: 45 Seconds.

Variations:

⊕ Double the target distance.

⊕ Any shooting position other than prone.

www.GUNFIGHTERSERIES.com ©

HEAD STRONG

Date:	Rifle:	Scope:	Dial Elev / Reticle Hold Over
Target Size:	Temp:	Humidity:	Baro:
Target 1 Range:	Elevation:	Windage:	Notes:
Target 2 Range:	Elevation:	Windage:	
Target 3 Range:	Elevation:	Windage:	
Target 4 Range:	Elevation:	Windage:	**Total Number of Shots:**
Target 5 Range:	Elevation:	Windage:	**Total Time:**
Date:	Rifle:	Scope:	Dial Elev / Reticle Hold Over
Target Size:	Temp:	Humidity:	Baro:
Target 1 Range:	Elevation:	Windage:	Notes:
Target 2 Range:	Elevation:	Windage:	
Target 3 Range:	Elevation:	Windage:	
Target 4 Range:	Elevation:	Windage:	**Total Number of Shots:**
Target 5 Range:	Elevation:	Windage:	**Total Time:**
Date:	Rifle:	Scope:	Dial Elev / Reticle Hold Over
Target Size:	Temp:	Humidity:	Baro:
Target 1 Range:	Elevation:	Windage:	Notes:
Target 2 Range:	Elevation:	Windage:	
Target 3 Range:	Elevation:	Windage:	
Target 4 Range:	Elevation:	Windage:	**Total Number of Shots:**
Target 5 Range:	Elevation:	Windage:	**Total Time:**

Multi Target Drills - 2

Precision Rifle ©

HEAD STRONG

www.GUNFIGHTERSERIES.com ©

Date:	Rifle:	Scope:	Dial Elev / Reticle Hold Over
Target Size:	Temp:	Humidity:	Baro:
Target 1 Range:	Elevation:	Windage:	Notes:
Target 2 Range:	Elevation:	Windage:	
Target 3 Range:	Elevation:	Windage:	
Target 4 Range:	Elevation:	Windage:	**Total Number of Shots:**
Target 5 Range:	Elevation:	Windage:	**Total Time:**
Date:	Rifle:	Scope:	Dial Elev / Reticle Hold Over
Target Size:	Temp:	Humidity:	Baro:
Target 1 Range:	Elevation:	Windage:	Notes:
Target 2 Range:	Elevation:	Windage:	
Target 3 Range:	Elevation:	Windage:	
Target 4 Range:	Elevation:	Windage:	**Total Number of Shots:**
Target 5 Range:	Elevation:	Windage:	**Total Time:**
Date:	Rifle:	Scope:	Dial Elev / Reticle Hold Over
Target Size:	Temp:	Humidity:	Baro:
Target 1 Range:	Elevation:	Windage:	Notes:
Target 2 Range:	Elevation:	Windage:	
Target 3 Range:	Elevation:	Windage:	
Target 4 Range:	Elevation:	Windage:	**Total Number of Shots:**
Target 5 Range:	Elevation:	Windage:	**Total Time:**

HEAD STRONG

Date:	Rifle:	Scope:	Dial Elev / Reticle Hold Over
Target Size:	Temp:	Humidity:	Baro:
Target 1 Range:	Elevation:	Windage:	Notes:
Target 2 Range:	Elevation:	Windage:	
Target 3 Range:	Elevation:	Windage:	
Target 4 Range:	Elevation:	Windage:	Total Number of Shots:
Target 5 Range:	Elevation:	Windage:	Total Time:
Date:	Rifle:	Scope:	Dial Elev / Reticle Hold Over
Target Size:	Temp:	Humidity:	Baro:
Target 1 Range:	Elevation:	Windage:	Notes:
Target 2 Range:	Elevation:	Windage:	
Target 3 Range:	Elevation:	Windage:	
Target 4 Range:	Elevation:	Windage:	Total Number of Shots:
Target 5 Range:	Elevation:	Windage:	Total Time:
Date:	Rifle:	Scope:	Dial Elev / Reticle Hold Over
Target Size:	Temp:	Humidity:	Baro:
Target 1 Range:	Elevation:	Windage:	Notes:
Target 2 Range:	Elevation:	Windage:	
Target 3 Range:	Elevation:	Windage:	
Target 4 Range:	Elevation:	Windage:	Total Number of Shots:
Target 5 Range:	Elevation:	Windage:	Total Time:

Multi Target Drills - 2

HEAD STRONG

www.GUNFIGHTERSERIES.com ©

Date:	Rifle:	Scope:	Dial Elev / Reticle Hold Over
Target Size:	Temp:	Humidity:	Baro:
Target 1 Range:	Elevation:	Windage:	Notes:
Target 2 Range:	Elevation:	Windage:	
Target 3 Range:	Elevation:	Windage:	
Target 4 Range:	Elevation:	Windage:	**Total Number of Shots:**
Target 5 Range:	Elevation:	Windage:	**Total Time:**
Date:	Rifle:	Scope:	Dial Elev / Reticle Hold Over
Target Size:	Temp:	Humidity:	Baro:
Target 1 Range:	Elevation:	Windage:	Notes:
Target 2 Range:	Elevation:	Windage:	
Target 3 Range:	Elevation:	Windage:	
Target 4 Range:	Elevation:	Windage:	**Total Number of Shots:**
Target 5 Range:	Elevation:	Windage:	**Total Time:**
Date:	Rifle:	Scope:	Dial Elev / Reticle Hold Over
Target Size:	Temp:	Humidity:	Baro:
Target 1 Range:	Elevation:	Windage:	Notes:
Target 2 Range:	Elevation:	Windage:	
Target 3 Range:	Elevation:	Windage:	
Target 4 Range:	Elevation:	Windage:	**Total Number of Shots:**
Target 5 Range:	Elevation:	Windage:	**Total Time:**

HEAD STRONG

Date:	Rifle:	Scope:	Dial Elev / Reticle Hold Over
Target Size:	Temp:	Humidity:	Baro:
Target 1 Range:	Elevation:	Windage:	Notes:
Target 2 Range:	Elevation:	Windage:	
Target 3 Range:	Elevation:	Windage:	
Target 4 Range:	Elevation:	Windage:	**Total Number of Shots:**
Target 5 Range:	Elevation:	Windage:	**Total Time:**
Date:	Rifle:	Scope:	Dial Elev / Reticle Hold Over
Target Size:	Temp:	Humidity:	Baro:
Target 1 Range:	Elevation:	Windage:	Notes:
Target 2 Range:	Elevation:	Windage:	
Target 3 Range:	Elevation:	Windage:	
Target 4 Range:	Elevation:	Windage:	**Total Number of Shots:**
Target 5 Range:	Elevation:	Windage:	**Total Time:**
Date:	Rifle:	Scope:	Dial Elev / Reticle Hold Over
Target Size:	Temp:	Humidity:	Baro:
Target 1 Range:	Elevation:	Windage:	Notes:
Target 2 Range:	Elevation:	Windage:	
Target 3 Range:	Elevation:	Windage:	
Target 4 Range:	Elevation:	Windage:	**Total Number of Shots:**
Target 5 Range:	Elevation:	Windage:	**Total Time:**

Multi Target Drills - 2

Precision Rifle ©

UP AND UP

Purpose: Reticle hold over familiarization.

Distance: 100, 200, 300, 400 and 500 yards.

Target: Steel silhouette targets X 5

Extra Equipment Needed: Shot timer. Shooting partner with spotting scope.

Total Rounds Fired: 10 Rounds.

Point Penalty: Time plus penalty. Add 20 seconds for each miss.

Repetitions: 1 Rep.

Starting Position & Condition: Standing behind rifle. Condition 1. Scope on personal rifle ZERO.

Description: Record current atmospherics, hold overs for each target distance and wind compensation for a 5 & 10 MPH wind at each target distance. Use the reticle to diagram your hold overs. (Shooting partner records hit placements and wind calls.)

At the timer beep, establish a good prone position, engage each target with 2 rounds each from closest to furthest without adjusting your scope turrets.

Add 20 seconds for each miss.

Goals: Novice: 150 Seconds. Expert: 100 Seconds. Gunfighter: 75 Seconds.

Variations: Engage targets in reverse order; far to near. Try different supported and unsupported shooting positions.

www.GUNFIGHTERSERIES.com ©

UP AND UP

Date:	Rifle:	Scope:
Ammo:	Near to Far / Far to Near	
MV:	Temp:	Baro:
Tgt 1 Elevation:	5 MPH:	10 MPH:
Tgt 2 Elevation:	5 MPH:	10 MPH:
Tgt 3 Elevation:	5 MPH:	10 MPH:
Tgt 4 Elevation:	5 MPH:	10 MPH:
Tgt 5 Elevation:	5 MPH:	10 MPH:
Prone / Sitting / Kneeling / Standing	Supported / Unsupported	
Target 1	1st Round Hit: Y / N	2nd Round Hit: Y / N
Target 2	1st Round Hit: Y / N	2nd Round Hit: Y / N
Target 3	1st Round Hit: Y / N	2nd Round Hit: Y / N
Target 4	1st Round Hit: Y / N	2nd Round Hit: Y / N
Target 5	1st Round Hit: Y / N	2nd Round Hit: Y / N
Rep Time:	# of Misses:	Total Time Score:
Notes:		

Multi Target Drills - 3

UP AND UP

Date:	Rifle:	Scope:
Ammo:	Near to Far / Far to Near	
MV:	Temp:	Baro:
Tgt 1 Elevation:	5 MPH:	10 MPH:
Tgt 2 Elevation:	5 MPH:	10 MPH:
Tgt 3 Elevation:	5 MPH:	10 MPH:
Tgt 4 Elevation:	5 MPH:	10 MPH:
Tgt 5 Elevation:	5 MPH:	10 MPH:
Prone / Sitting / Kneeling / Standing		Supported / Unsupported
Target 1	1st Round Hit: Y / N	2nd Round Hit: Y / N
Target 2	1st Round Hit: Y / N	2nd Round Hit: Y / N
Target 3	1st Round Hit: Y / N	2nd Round Hit: Y / N
Target 4	1st Round Hit: Y / N	2nd Round Hit: Y / N
Target 5	1st Round Hit: Y / N	2nd Round Hit: Y / N
Rep Time:	# of Misses:	Total Time Score:
Notes:		

UP AND UP

Date:	Rifle:	Scope:
Ammo:	Near to Far / Far to Near	
MV:	Temp:	Baro:
Tgt 1 Elevation:	5 MPH:	10 MPH:
Tgt 2 Elevation:	5 MPH:	10 MPH:
Tgt 3 Elevation:	5 MPH:	10 MPH:
Tgt 4 Elevation:	5 MPH:	10 MPH:
Tgt 5 Elevation:	5 MPH:	10 MPH:
Prone / Sitting / Kneeling / Standing	Supported / Unsupported	
Target 1	1st Round Hit: Y / N	2nd Round Hit: Y / N
Target 2	1st Round Hit: Y / N	2nd Round Hit: Y / N
Target 3	1st Round Hit: Y / N	2nd Round Hit: Y / N
Target 4	1st Round Hit: Y / N	2nd Round Hit: Y / N
Target 5	1st Round Hit: Y / N	2nd Round Hit: Y / N
Rep Time:	# of Misses:	Total Time Score:
Notes:		

Multi Target Drills - 3

UP AND UP

Date:	Rifle:	Scope:
Ammo:	Near to Far / Far to Near	
MV:	Temp:	Baro:
Tgt 1 Elevation:	5 MPH:	10 MPH:
Tgt 2 Elevation:	5 MPH:	10 MPH:
Tgt 3 Elevation:	5 MPH:	10 MPH:
Tgt 4 Elevation:	5 MPH:	10 MPH:
Tgt 5 Elevation:	5 MPH:	10 MPH:
Prone / Sitting / Kneeling / Standing	Supported / Unsupported	
Target 1	1st Round Hit: Y / N	2nd Round Hit: Y / N
Target 2	1st Round Hit: Y / N	2nd Round Hit: Y / N
Target 3	1st Round Hit: Y / N	2nd Round Hit: Y / N
Target 4	1st Round Hit: Y / N	2nd Round Hit: Y / N
Target 5	1st Round Hit: Y / N	2nd Round Hit: Y / N
Rep Time:	# of Misses:	Total Time Score:
Notes:		

UP AND UP

MIL

MOA

Date:	Rifle:	Scope:
Ammo:	Near to Far / Far to Near	
MV:	Temp:	Baro:
Tgt 1 Elevation:	5 MPH:	10 MPH:
Tgt 2 Elevation:	5 MPH:	10 MPH:
Tgt 3 Elevation:	5 MPH:	10 MPH:
Tgt 4 Elevation:	5 MPH:	10 MPH:
Tgt 5 Elevation:	5 MPH:	10 MPH:
Prone / Sitting / Kneeling / Standing	Supported / Unsupported	
Target 1	1st Round Hit: Y / N	2nd Round Hit: Y / N
Target 2	1st Round Hit: Y / N	2nd Round Hit: Y / N
Target 3	1st Round Hit: Y / N	2nd Round Hit: Y / N
Target 4	1st Round Hit: Y / N	2nd Round Hit: Y / N
Target 5	1st Round Hit: Y / N	2nd Round Hit: Y / N
Rep Time:	# of Misses:	Total Time Score:
Notes:		

Multi Target Drills - 3

Precision Rifle ©

GOING THE DISTANCE

Purpose: Accuracy with multiple targets.

Distance: Close range (100-300). Mid range (400-600). Long range (700-1000+) yards.

Target: Random steel targets X 3. (1 Close range. 1 Mid range. 1 Long range.)

Par Time: 90 Seconds.

Extra Equipment Needed: Shot timer. Shooting partner with spotting scope.

Total Rounds Fired: 6 Rounds.

Point Penalty: 1st round hit = 10 points. 2nd round hit = 5 points. Miss = 0 points.

Repetitions: 1 Reps.

Starting Position & Condition: Standing behind rifle. Condition 1. Scope on personal rifle ZERO.

Description: Record current temperature, range to target, elevation and average wind adjustment needed. (Shooting partner records hit placements and wind calls.)

At the timer beep, establish a good prone position, dial or hold over for the closest target then engage with 2 rounds. Acquire mid range target, dial or hold over for the mid range target then engage with 2 rounds. Acquire long range target, dial or hold over for the long range target then engage with 2 rounds.

Goals: Novice: 25 points under par.   Expert: 45 points under par.   Gunfighter: 45 points under a 60 second par.

Variations: Dial elevation turret or use a reticle hold over. Try engaging targets in reverse order; far to near.

GOING THE DISTANCE

Date:	Rifle:	Hold Over / Dial Elev	Near to Far / Far to Near
Close Distance:	**Mid Distance:**	**Long Distance:**	Under Par: Y / N
1st Round Hit: Y / N	1st Round Hit: Y / N	1st Round Hit: Y / N	Time:
2nd Round Hit: Y / N	2nd Round Hit: Y / N	2nd Round Hit: Y / N	**Score:**

Date:	Rifle:	Hold Over / Dial Elev	Near to Far / Far to Near
Close Distance:	**Mid Distance:**	**Long Distance:**	Under Par: Y / N
1st Round Hit: Y / N	1st Round Hit: Y / N	1st Round Hit: Y / N	Time:
2nd Round Hit: Y / N	2nd Round Hit: Y / N	2nd Round Hit: Y / N	**Score:**

Date:	Rifle:	Hold Over / Dial Elev	Near to Far / Far to Near
Close Distance:	**Mid Distance:**	**Long Distance:**	Under Par: Y / N
1st Round Hit: Y / N	1st Round Hit: Y / N	1st Round Hit: Y / N	Time:
2nd Round Hit: Y / N	2nd Round Hit: Y / N	2nd Round Hit: Y / N	**Score:**

Precision Rifle ©

Multi Target Drills - 4

GOING THE DISTANCE

Date:	Rifle:	Hold Over / Dial Elev	Near to Far / Far to Near
Close Distance:	**Mid Distance:**	**Long Distance:**	Under Par: Y / N
1st Round Hit: Y / N	1st Round Hit: Y / N	1st Round Hit: Y / N	Time:
2nd Round Hit: Y / N	2nd Round Hit: Y / N	2nd Round Hit: Y / N	**Score:**

Date:	Rifle:	Hold Over / Dial Elev	Near to Far / Far to Near
Close Distance:	**Mid Distance:**	**Long Distance:**	Under Par: Y / N
1st Round Hit: Y / N	1st Round Hit: Y / N	1st Round Hit: Y / N	Time:
2nd Round Hit: Y / N	2nd Round Hit: Y / N	2nd Round Hit: Y / N	**Score:**

Date:	Rifle:	Hold Over / Dial Elev	Near to Far / Far to Near
Close Distance:	**Mid Distance:**	**Long Distance:**	Under Par: Y / N
1st Round Hit: Y / N	1st Round Hit: Y / N	1st Round Hit: Y / N	Time:
2nd Round Hit: Y / N	2nd Round Hit: Y / N	2nd Round Hit: Y / N	**Score:**

www.GUNFIGHTERSERIES.com ©

GOING THE DISTANCE

Date:	Rifle:	Hold Over / Dial Elev	Near to Far / Far to Near
Close Distance:	Mid Distance:	Long Distance:	Under Par: Y / N
1st Round Hit: Y / N	1st Round Hit: Y / N	1st Round Hit: Y / N	Time:
2nd Round Hit: Y / N	2nd Round Hit: Y / N	2nd Round Hit: Y / N	Score:

Date:	Rifle:	Hold Over / Dial Elev	Near to Far / Far to Near
Close Distance:	Mid Distance:	Long Distance:	Under Par: Y / N
1st Round Hit: Y / N	1st Round Hit: Y / N	1st Round Hit: Y / N	Time:
2nd Round Hit: Y / N	2nd Round Hit: Y / N	2nd Round Hit: Y / N	Score:

Date:	Rifle:	Hold Over / Dial Elev	Near to Far / Far to Near
Close Distance:	Mid Distance:	Long Distance:	Under Par: Y / N
1st Round Hit: Y / N	1st Round Hit: Y / N	1st Round Hit: Y / N	Time:
2nd Round Hit: Y / N	2nd Round Hit: Y / N	2nd Round Hit: Y / N	Score:

Precision Rifle ©

Multi Target Drills - 4

GOING THE DISTANCE

Date:	Rifle:	Hold Over / Dial Elev	Near to Far / Far to Near
Close Distance:	**Mid Distance:**	**Long Distance:**	Under Par: Y / N
1st Round Hit: Y / N	1st Round Hit: Y / N	1st Round Hit: Y / N	Time:
2nd Round Hit: Y / N	2nd Round Hit: Y / N	2nd Round Hit: Y / N	**Score:**

Date:	Rifle:	Hold Over / Dial Elev	Near to Far / Far to Near
Close Distance:	**Mid Distance:**	**Long Distance:**	Under Par: Y / N
1st Round Hit: Y / N	1st Round Hit: Y / N	1st Round Hit: Y / N	Time:
2nd Round Hit: Y / N	2nd Round Hit: Y / N	2nd Round Hit: Y / N	**Score:**

Date:	Rifle:	Hold Over / Dial Elev	Near to Far / Far to Near
Close Distance:	**Mid Distance:**	**Long Distance:**	Under Par: Y / N
1st Round Hit: Y / N	1st Round Hit: Y / N	1st Round Hit: Y / N	Time:
2nd Round Hit: Y / N	2nd Round Hit: Y / N	2nd Round Hit: Y / N	**Score:**

www.GUNFIGHTERSERIES.com ©

GOING THE DISTANCE

Date:	Rifle:	Hold Over / Dial Elev	Near to Far / Far to Near
Close Distance:	**Mid Distance:**	**Long Distance:**	Under Par: Y / N
1st Round Hit: Y / N	1st Round Hit: Y / N	1st Round Hit: Y / N	Time:
2nd Round Hit: Y / N	2nd Round Hit: Y / N	2nd Round Hit: Y / N	**Score:**

Date:	Rifle:	Hold Over / Dial Elev	Near to Far / Far to Near
Close Distance:	**Mid Distance:**	**Long Distance:**	Under Par: Y / N
1st Round Hit: Y / N	1st Round Hit: Y / N	1st Round Hit: Y / N	Time:
2nd Round Hit: Y / N	2nd Round Hit: Y / N	2nd Round Hit: Y / N	**Score:**

Date:	Rifle:	Hold Over / Dial Elev	Near to Far / Far to Near
Close Distance:	**Mid Distance:**	**Long Distance:**	Under Par: Y / N
1st Round Hit: Y / N	1st Round Hit: Y / N	1st Round Hit: Y / N	Time:
2nd Round Hit: Y / N	2nd Round Hit: Y / N	2nd Round Hit: Y / N	**Score:**

Multi Target Drills - 4

Precision Rifle ©

ONE AND DONE

Purpose: Multiple target engagement speed and transitioning.

Distance: 300, 500, 700 yards.

Target: Steel targets X 3.

Extra Equipment Needed: Shot timer. Shooting partner with spotting scope.

Total Rounds Fired: 3 to 10 Rounds.

Point Penalty: Hit / Miss.

Repetitions: 1 Rep.

Starting Position & Condition: Prone, aimed in. Condition 1.

Description: Record current temperature, range to target, elevation and average wind adjustment needed. (Shooting partner records hit placements and wind calls.)

At the timer beep, take weapon off safe and fire one round at the 300 yard target. If you hit, transition to the 500 yard target. If you miss then reengage the same target. If you hit, transition to the 700 yard target. If you miss then reengage the same target. If you hit the target then the drill is complete.

Goals: Novice: 25 Seconds.   Expert: 12.5 Seconds.   Gunfighter: 7.5 Seconds.

Variations: Dial elevation turret or use a reticle hold over. Try engaging targets in reverse order; far to near.

ONE AND DONE

Date:	Rifle:	Scope:	Hold Over / Dial Elev
MV:	Temp:	Baro:	Near to Far / Far to Near
300 Elevation:	500 Elevation:	700 Elevation:	Notes:
# of shots:	# of misses:	Total Time:	

Date:	Rifle:	Scope:	Hold Over / Dial Elev
MV:	Temp:	Baro:	Near to Far / Far to Near
300 Elevation:	500 Elevation:	700 Elevation:	Notes:
# of shots:	# of misses:	Total Time:	

Date:	Rifle:	Scope:	Hold Over / Dial Elev
MV:	Temp:	Baro:	Near to Far / Far to Near
300 Elevation:	500 Elevation:	700 Elevation:	Notes:
# of shots:	# of misses:	Total Time:	

Precision Rifle ©

Multi Target Drills - 5

ONE AND DONE

www.GUNFIGHTERSERIES.com ©

Date:	Rifle:	Scope:	Hold Over / Dial Elev
MV:	Temp:	Baro:	Near to Far / Far to Near
300 Elevation:	500 Elevation:	700 Elevation:	Notes:
# of shots:	# of misses:	Total Time:	

Date:	Rifle:	Scope:	Hold Over / Dial Elev
MV:	Temp:	Baro:	Near to Far / Far to Near
300 Elevation:	500 Elevation:	700 Elevation:	Notes:
# of shots:	# of misses:	Total Time:	

Date:	Rifle:	Scope:	Hold Over / Dial Elev
MV:	Temp:	Baro:	Near to Far / Far to Near
300 Elevation:	500 Elevation:	700 Elevation:	Notes:
# of shots:	# of misses:	Total Time:	

ONE AND DONE

Date:	Rifle:	Scope:	Hold Over / Dial Elev
MV:	Temp:	Baro:	Near to Far / Far to Near
300 Elevation:	500 Elevation:	700 Elevation:	Notes:
# of shots:	# of misses:	Total Time:	

Date:	Rifle:	Scope:	Hold Over / Dial Elev
MV:	Temp:	Baro:	Near to Far / Far to Near
300 Elevation:	500 Elevation:	700 Elevation:	Notes:
# of shots:	# of misses:	Total Time:	

Date:	Rifle:	Scope:	Hold Over / Dial Elev
MV:	Temp:	Baro:	Near to Far / Far to Near
300 Elevation:	500 Elevation:	700 Elevation:	Notes:
# of shots:	# of misses:	Total Time:	

Precision Rifle ©

Multi Target Drills - 5

ONE AND DONE

www.GUNFIGHTERSERIES.com ©

Date:	Rifle:	Scope:	Hold Over / Dial Elev
MV:	Temp:	Baro:	Near to Far / Far to Near
300 Elevation:	500 Elevation:	700 Elevation:	Notes:
# of shots:	# of misses:	Total Time:	

Date:	Rifle:	Scope:	Hold Over / Dial Elev
MV:	Temp:	Baro:	Near to Far / Far to Near
300 Elevation:	500 Elevation:	700 Elevation:	Notes:
# of shots:	# of misses:	Total Time:	

Date:	Rifle:	Scope:	Hold Over / Dial Elev
MV:	Temp:	Baro:	Near to Far / Far to Near
300 Elevation:	500 Elevation:	700 Elevation:	Notes:
# of shots:	# of misses:	Total Time:	

ONE AND DONE

Date:	Rifle:	Scope:	Hold Over / Dial Elev
MV:	Temp:	Baro:	Near to Far / Far to Near
300 Elevation:	500 Elevation:	700 Elevation:	Notes:
# of shots:	# of misses:	Total Time:	

Date:	Rifle:	Scope:	Hold Over / Dial Elev
MV:	Temp:	Baro:	Near to Far / Far to Near
300 Elevation:	500 Elevation:	700 Elevation:	Notes:
# of shots:	# of misses:	Total Time:	

Date:	Rifle:	Scope:	Hold Over / Dial Elev
MV:	Temp:	Baro:	Near to Far / Far to Near
300 Elevation:	500 Elevation:	700 Elevation:	Notes:
# of shots:	# of misses:	Total Time:	

Multi Target Drills - 5

Precision Rifle ©

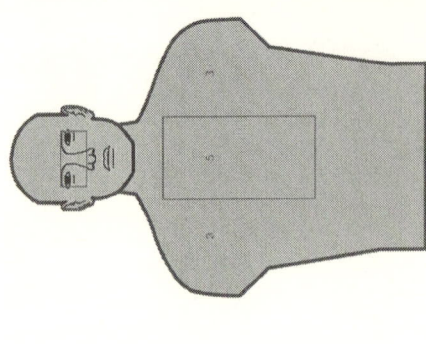

REAL WORLD COLD BORE

Purpose: Test shooters ability to adjust for cold bore offset in real world conditions.

Distance: 50 - 300 Yards. (Let your shooting partner place so you do not know the actual distance.)

Target: JD-QUAL1

Extra Equipment Needed: Shot timer. 1 Barricade. Standard equipment loadout.

Total Rounds Fired: 1 Round.

Point Penalty: Go / No Go.

Starting Position & Condition: Standing. Condition 4.

Description: Record atmospherics and turret settings if on ZERO or adjusted for CB (Cold Bore) / CCB (Clean Cold Bore). Stage rifle in a safe manner in condition 4 at the firing line next to the prescribed barricade. Begin drill by jogging for no less than 5 minutes. Upon returning, immediately start the 30 second countdown. At the timer beep, make elevation scope turret adjustment as needed, create any stable firing position (other than prone) using provided support, load rifle with 1 round then fire 1 round into the 5 point head A zone box.

Goals: Novice: Head A box hit under 60 seconds.   Expert: Head A box hit under 45 seconds.   Gunfighter: Head A box hit under 30 seconds.

Variations: Mix up this drill each time with different target distances, angle to target, types of barricades and shooting positions.

www.GUNFIGHTERSERIES.com ©

REAL WORLD COLD BORE

Date:	Rifle		Scope:		Ammo:
Temp:	Baro:		CB / CCB		Notes:
Range To Target:	Elev:	Wind:	Angle:	Cosign:	
Barricade:	Sitting / Kneeling / Standing		**Go / No Go**		**Time:**
Date:	Rifle		Scope:		Ammo:
Temp:	Baro:		CB / CCB		Notes:
Range To Target:	Elev:	Wind:	Angle:	Cosign:	
Barricade:	Sitting / Kneeling / Standing		**Go / No Go**		**Time:**
Date:	Rifle		Scope:		Ammo:
Temp:	Baro:		CB / CCB		Notes:
Range To Target:	Elev:	Wind:	Angle:	Cosign:	
Barricade:	Sitting / Kneeling / Standing		**Go / No Go**		**Time:**
Date:	Rifle		Scope:		Ammo:
Temp:	Baro:		CB / CCB		Notes:
Range To Target:	Elev:	Wind:	Angle:	Cosign:	
Barricade:	Sitting / Kneeling / Standing		**Go / No Go**		**Time:**

REAL WORLD COLD BORE

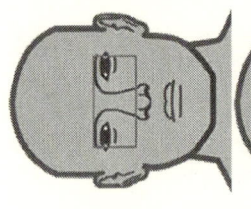

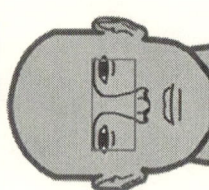

www.GUNFIGHTERSERIES.com ©

Date:	Rifle:	Scope:	Ammo:
Temp:	Baro:	CB / CCB	Notes:
Range To Target:	Elev: Wind:	Angle: Cosign:	
Barricade:	Sitting / Kneeling / Standing	**Go / No Go**	**Time:**

Date:	Rifle:	Scope:	Ammo:
Temp:	Baro:	CB / CCB	Notes:
Range To Target:	Elev: Wind:	Angle: Cosign:	
Barricade:	Sitting / Kneeling / Standing	**Go / No Go**	**Time:**

Date:	Rifle:	Scope:	Ammo:
Temp:	Baro:	CB / CCB	Notes:
Range To Target:	Elev: Wind:	Angle: Cosign:	
Barricade:	Sitting / Kneeling / Standing	**Go / No Go**	**Time:**

Date:	Rifle:	Scope:	Ammo:
Temp:	Baro:	CB / CCB	Notes:
Range To Target:	Elev: Wind:	Angle: Cosign:	
Barricade:	Sitting / Kneeling / Standing	**Go / No Go**	**Time:**

REAL WORLD COLD BORE

Date:	Rifle	Scope:	Ammo:
Temp:	Baro:	CB / CCB	Notes:
Range To Target:	Elev: Wind:	Angle: Cosign:	
Barricade:	Sitting / Kneeling / Standing	**Go / No Go**	**Time:**
Date:	Rifle	Scope:	Ammo:
Temp:	Baro:	CB / CCB	Notes:
Range To Target:	Elev: Wind:	Angle: Cosign:	
Barricade:	Sitting / Kneeling / Standing	**Go / No Go**	**Time:**
Date:	Rifle	Scope:	Ammo:
Temp:	Baro:	CB / CCB	Notes:
Range To Target:	Elev: Wind:	Angle: Cosign:	
Barricade:	Sitting / Kneeling / Standing	**Go / No Go**	**Time:**
Date:	Rifle	Scope:	Ammo:
Temp:	Baro:	CB / CCB	Notes:
Range To Target:	Elev: Wind:	Angle: Cosign:	
Barricade:	Sitting / Kneeling / Standing	**Go / No Go**	**Time:**

Precision Rifle ©

Gunfighter Drills - 1

REAL WORLD COLD BORE

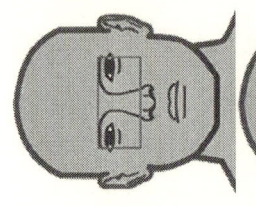   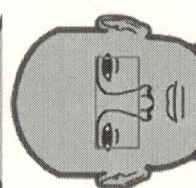

Date:	Rifle	Scope:	Ammo:
Temp:	Baro:	CB / CCB	Notes:
Range To Target:	Elev: Wind:	Angle: Cosign:	
Barricade:	Sitting / Kneeling / Standing	**Go / No Go**	Time:
Date:	Rifle	Scope:	Ammo:
Temp:	Baro:	CB / CCB	Notes:
Range To Target:	Elev: Wind:	Angle: Cosign:	
Barricade:	Sitting / Kneeling / Standing	**Go / No Go**	Time:
Date:	Rifle	Scope:	Ammo:
Temp:	Baro:	CB / CCB	Notes:
Range To Target:	Elev: Wind:	Angle: Cosign:	
Barricade:	Sitting / Kneeling / Standing	**Go / No Go**	Time:
Date:	Rifle	Scope:	Ammo:
Temp:	Baro:	CB / CCB	Notes:
Range To Target:	Elev: Wind:	Angle: Cosign:	
Barricade:	Sitting / Kneeling / Standing	**Go / No Go**	Time:

www.GUNFIGHTERSERIES.com ©

REAL WORLD COLD BORE

Date:	Rifle		Scope:		Ammo:
Temp:	Baro:		CB / CCB		Notes:
Range To Target:	Elev:	Wind:	Angle:	Cosign:	
Barricade:	Sitting / Kneeling / Standing			Go / No Go	Time:
Date:	Rifle		Scope:		Ammo:
Temp:	Baro:		CB / CCB		Notes:
Range To Target:	Elev:	Wind:	Angle:	Cosign:	
Barricade:	Sitting / Kneeling / Standing			Go / No Go	Time:
Date:	Rifle		Scope:		Ammo:
Temp:	Baro:		CB / CCB		Notes:
Range To Target:	Elev:	Wind:	Angle:	Cosign:	
Barricade:	Sitting / Kneeling / Standing			Go / No Go	Time:
Date:	Rifle		Scope:		Ammo:
Temp:	Baro:		CB / CCB		Notes:
Range To Target:	Elev:	Wind:	Angle:	Cosign:	
Barricade:	Sitting / Kneeling / Standing			Go / No Go	Time:

Gunfighter Drills - 1

Precision Rifle ©

BURPEE BATTLE

Purpose: Increase target transition speed while maintaining NPA and target acquisition speed.

By: Francis Colon

Distance: Per goal standards.

Target: Steel circle, or head silhouette, targets no larger than 8 inches.

Par Time: Per goal standards.

Extra Equipment Needed: Shot timer.

Rounds Fired Per Rep: 5 Rounds.

Point Penalty: 1 Point per impact.

Repetitions: 3 Reps.

Starting Position & Condition: Standing - Rifle placed on firing line. Condition 1.

Total Rounds Fired: 15 Rounds.

Description: At the timer beep, assume a good prone position, and engage the target with 1 round. Put rifle on safe and stand up with hands over your head (burpee), and then assume a good prone position to reengage the same target. Continue conducting 1 burpee between each shot for a total of 5 shots fired. Any miss or over goal par time is a failure.

Goals: Novice: 60 Second reps at 200 yards. Expert: 50 Second reps at 300 yards. Gunfighter: 45 Second reps at 400 yards.

Variations: Use 3 targets. Engage in order of 200y, 300y, 400, 300y, and 200y with 1 burpee between each shot. Same goal par times.

BURPEE BATTLE

Date:	Rifle:	Scope:	Dial Elev / Hold Over	Notes:
Target Distance:	Rep 1 Time:	Rep 2 Time:	Rep 3 Time:	
Target Size:	Rep 1 Score:	Rep 2 Score:	Rep 3 Score:	

Date:	Rifle:	Scope:	Dial Elev / Hold Over	Notes:
Target Distance:	Rep 1 Time:	Rep 2 Time:	Rep 3 Time:	
Target Size:	Rep 1 Score:	Rep 2 Score:	Rep 3 Score:	

Date:	Rifle:	Scope:	Dial Elev / Hold Over	Notes:
Target Distance:	Rep 1 Time:	Rep 2 Time:	Rep 3 Time:	
Target Size:	Rep 1 Score:	Rep 2 Score:	Rep 3 Score:	

Date:	Rifle:	Scope:	Dial Elev / Hold Over	Notes:
Target Distance:	Rep 1 Time:	Rep 2 Time:	Rep 3 Time:	
Target Size:	Rep 1 Score:	Rep 2 Score:	Rep 3 Score:	

Date:	Rifle:	Scope:	Dial Elev / Hold Over	Notes:
Target Distance:	Rep 1 Time:	Rep 2 Time:	Rep 3 Time:	
Target Size:	Rep 1 Score:	Rep 2 Score:	Rep 3 Score:	

Gunfighter Drills - 2

Precision Rifle ©

BURPEE BATTLE

Date:	Rifle:	Scope:	Dial Elev / Hold Over	Notes:
Target Distance:	Rep 1 Time:	Rep 2 Time:	Rep 3 Time:	
Target Size:	Rep 1 Score:	Rep 2 Score:	Rep 3 Score:	

Date:	Rifle:	Scope:	Dial Elev / Hold Over	Notes:
Target Distance:	Rep 1 Time:	Rep 2 Time:	Rep 3 Time:	
Target Size:	Rep 1 Score:	Rep 2 Score:	Rep 3 Score:	

Date:	Rifle:	Scope:	Dial Elev / Hold Over	Notes:
Target Distance:	Rep 1 Time:	Rep 2 Time:	Rep 3 Time:	
Target Size:	Rep 1 Score:	Rep 2 Score:	Rep 3 Score:	

Date:	Rifle:	Scope:	Dial Elev / Hold Over	Notes:
Target Distance:	Rep 1 Time:	Rep 2 Time:	Rep 3 Time:	
Target Size:	Rep 1 Score:	Rep 2 Score:	Rep 3 Score:	

Date:	Rifle:	Scope:	Dial Elev / Hold Over	Notes:
Target Distance:	Rep 1 Time:	Rep 2 Time:	Rep 3 Time:	
Target Size:	Rep 1 Score:	Rep 2 Score:	Rep 3 Score:	

BURPEE BATTLE

Date:	Rifle:	Scope:	Dial Elev / Hold Over	Notes:
Target Distance:		Rep 1 Time:	Rep 2 Time:	Rep 3 Time:	
Target Size:		Rep 1 Score:	Rep 2 Score:	Rep 3 Score:	

Date:	Rifle:	Scope:	Dial Elev / Hold Over	Notes:
Target Distance:		Rep 1 Time:	Rep 2 Time:	Rep 3 Time:	
Target Size:		Rep 1 Score:	Rep 2 Score:	Rep 3 Score:	

Date:	Rifle:	Scope:	Dial Elev / Hold Over	Notes:
Target Distance:		Rep 1 Time:	Rep 2 Time:	Rep 3 Time:	
Target Size:		Rep 1 Score:	Rep 2 Score:	Rep 3 Score:	

Date:	Rifle:	Scope:	Dial Elev / Hold Over	Notes:
Target Distance:		Rep 1 Time:	Rep 2 Time:	Rep 3 Time:	
Target Size:		Rep 1 Score:	Rep 2 Score:	Rep 3 Score:	

Date:	Rifle:	Scope:	Dial Elev / Hold Over	Notes:
Target Distance:		Rep 1 Time:	Rep 2 Time:	Rep 3 Time:	
Target Size:		Rep 1 Score:	Rep 2 Score:	Rep 3 Score:	

Gunfighter Drills - 2

Precision Rifle ©

BURPEE BATTLE

Date:	Rifle:	Scope:	Dial Elev / Hold Over	Notes:
Target Distance:	Rep 1 Time:	Rep 2 Time:	Rep 3 Time:	
Target Size:	Rep 1 Score:	Rep 2 Score:	Rep 3 Score:	

Date:	Rifle:	Scope:	Dial Elev / Hold Over	Notes:
Target Distance:	Rep 1 Time:	Rep 2 Time:	Rep 3 Time:	
Target Size:	Rep 1 Score:	Rep 2 Score:	Rep 3 Score:	

Date:	Rifle:	Scope:	Dial Elev / Hold Over	Notes:
Target Distance:	Rep 1 Time:	Rep 2 Time:	Rep 3 Time:	
Target Size:	Rep 1 Score:	Rep 2 Score:	Rep 3 Score:	

Date:	Rifle:	Scope:	Dial Elev / Hold Over	Notes:
Target Distance:	Rep 1 Time:	Rep 2 Time:	Rep 3 Time:	
Target Size:	Rep 1 Score:	Rep 2 Score:	Rep 3 Score:	

Date:	Rifle:	Scope:	Dial Elev / Hold Over	Notes:
Target Distance:	Rep 1 Time:	Rep 2 Time:	Rep 3 Time:	
Target Size:	Rep 1 Score:	Rep 2 Score:	Rep 3 Score:	

www.GUNFIGHTERSERIES.com ©

BURPEE BATTLE

Date:	Rifle:	Scope:	Dial Elev / Hold Over	Notes:
Target Distance:	Rep 1 Time:	Rep 2 Time:	Rep 3 Time:	
Target Size:	Rep 1 Score:	Rep 2 Score:	Rep 3 Score:	

Date:	Rifle:	Scope:	Dial Elev / Hold Over	Notes:
Target Distance:	Rep 1 Time:	Rep 2 Time:	Rep 3 Time:	
Target Size:	Rep 1 Score:	Rep 2 Score:	Rep 3 Score:	

Date:	Rifle:	Scope:	Dial Elev / Hold Over	Notes:
Target Distance:	Rep 1 Time:	Rep 2 Time:	Rep 3 Time:	
Target Size:	Rep 1 Score:	Rep 2 Score:	Rep 3 Score:	

Date:	Rifle:	Scope:	Dial Elev / Hold Over	Notes:
Target Distance:	Rep 1 Time:	Rep 2 Time:	Rep 3 Time:	
Target Size:	Rep 1 Score:	Rep 2 Score:	Rep 3 Score:	

Date:	Rifle:	Scope:	Dial Elev / Hold Over	Notes:
Target Distance:	Rep 1 Time:	Rep 2 Time:	Rep 3 Time:	
Target Size:	Rep 1 Score:	Rep 2 Score:	Rep 3 Score:	

Gunfighter Drills - 2

Precision Rifle ©

SNIPER PREZ

Purpose: Close range defensive shooting, mag changes, stress.

Distance: 25 Yards.

Target: JD-QUAL1 X 3

Extra Equipment Needed: Shot timer. 2 Mags with 3 rounds each. Mag pouch

Rounds Fired Per Rep: 6 Rounds.   **Total Rounds Fired:** 18 Rounds.

Point Penalty: As per target score.

Repetitions: 3 Reps.

Starting Position & Condition: Standing low ready. Condition 1.

Description: At the timer beep, engage each target from right to left with one round each. Reload. Reengage each target left to right with one round each to the A Zone (5 point) body box. Record time, score targets. For every hit in the 3 scoring zone, add 3 seconds to your time. For every hit in the 0 scoring zone, add 5 seconds to your time. Add the penalty time onto your recorded time for that repetition. Average all of the repetitions and there is your time.

NOTE: It's best to patrol with your rifle scope on it's lowest power setting.

Goals: Novice: 30 Seconds.   Expert: 20 Seconds.   Gunfighter: 17.5 Seconds.

SNIPER PREZ

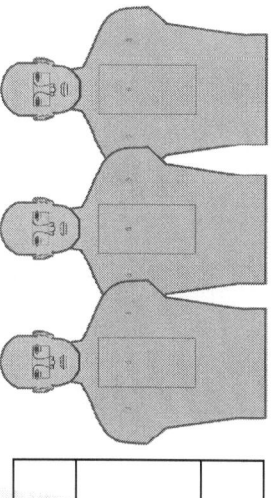
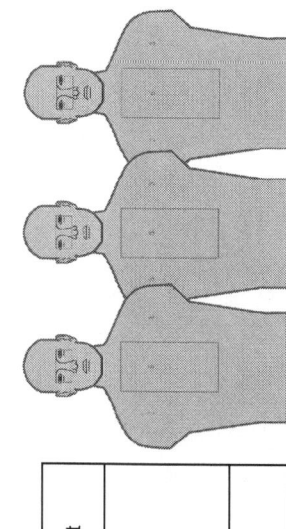

Date:	Location:	Rifle:	Scope / Micro Dot
Rep 1 Time:	Rep 2 Time:	Rep 3 Time:	Notes:
+ Penalties:	+ Penalties:	+ Penalties:	
= Rep 1 Score:	= Rep 2 Score:	= Rep 3 Score:	**Ave Rep Score:**

Date:	Location:	Rifle:	Scope / Micro Dot
Rep 1 Time:	Rep 2 Time:	Rep 3 Time:	Notes:
+ Penalties:	+ Penalties:	+ Penalties:	
= Rep 1 Score:	= Rep 2 Score:	= Rep 3 Score:	**Ave Rep Score:**

Date:	Location:	Rifle:	Scope / Micro Dot
Rep 1 Time:	Rep 2 Time:	Rep 3 Time:	Notes:
+ Penalties:	+ Penalties:	+ Penalties:	
= Rep 1 Score:	= Rep 2 Score:	= Rep 3 Score:	**Ave Rep Score:**

Gunfighter Drills - 3

Precision Rifle ©

SNIPER PREZ

www.GUNFIGHTERSERIES.com ©

Date:	Location:	Rifle:	Scope / Micro Dot
Rep 1 Time:	Rep 2 Time:	Rep 3 Time:	Notes:
+ Penalties:	+ Penalties:	+ Penalties:	
= Rep 1 Score:	= Rep 2 Score:	= Rep 3 Score:	**Ave Rep Score:**

Date:	Location:	Rifle:	Scope / Micro Dot
Rep 1 Time:	Rep 2 Time:	Rep 3 Time:	Notes:
+ Penalties:	+ Penalties:	+ Penalties:	
= Rep 1 Score:	= Rep 2 Score:	= Rep 3 Score:	**Ave Rep Score:**

Date:	Location:	Rifle:	Scope / Micro Dot
Rep 1 Time:	Rep 2 Time:	Rep 3 Time:	Notes:
+ Penalties:	+ Penalties:	+ Penalties:	
= Rep 1 Score:	= Rep 2 Score:	= Rep 3 Score:	**Ave Rep Score:**

SNIPER PREZ

Date:	Location:	Rifle:	Scope / Micro Dot
Rep 1 Time:	Rep 2 Time:	Rep 3 Time:	Notes:
+ Penalties:	+ Penalties:	+ Penalties:	
= Rep 1 Score:	= Rep 2 Score:	= Rep 3 Score:	Ave Rep Score:

Date:	Location:	Rifle:	Scope / Micro Dot
Rep 1 Time:	Rep 2 Time:	Rep 3 Time:	Notes:
+ Penalties:	+ Penalties:	+ Penalties:	
= Rep 1 Score:	= Rep 2 Score:	= Rep 3 Score:	Ave Rep Score:

Date:	Location:	Rifle:	Scope / Micro Dot
Rep 1 Time:	Rep 2 Time:	Rep 3 Time:	Notes:
+ Penalties:	+ Penalties:	+ Penalties:	
= Rep 1 Score:	= Rep 2 Score:	= Rep 3 Score:	Ave Rep Score:

SNIPER PREZ

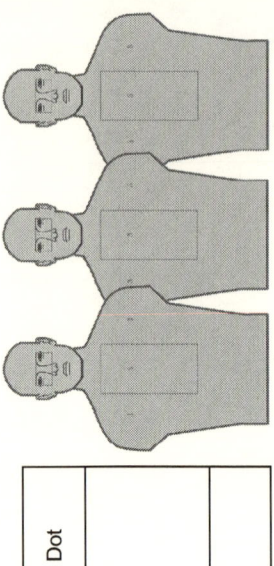

Date:	Location:	Rifle:	Scope / Micro Dot
Rep 1 Time:	Rep 2 Time:	Rep 3 Time:	Notes:
+ Penalties:	+ Penalties:	+ Penalties:	
= Rep 1 Score:	= Rep 2 Score:	= Rep 3 Score:	**Ave Rep Score:**

Date:	Location:	Rifle:	Scope / Micro Dot
Rep 1 Time:	Rep 2 Time:	Rep 3 Time:	Notes:
+ Penalties:	+ Penalties:	+ Penalties:	
= Rep 1 Score:	= Rep 2 Score:	= Rep 3 Score:	**Ave Rep Score:**

Date:	Location:	Rifle:	Scope / Micro Dot
Rep 1 Time:	Rep 2 Time:	Rep 3 Time:	Notes:
+ Penalties:	+ Penalties:	+ Penalties:	
= Rep 1 Score:	= Rep 2 Score:	= Rep 3 Score:	**Ave Rep Score:**

www.GUNFIGHTERSERIES.com ©

SNIPER PREZ

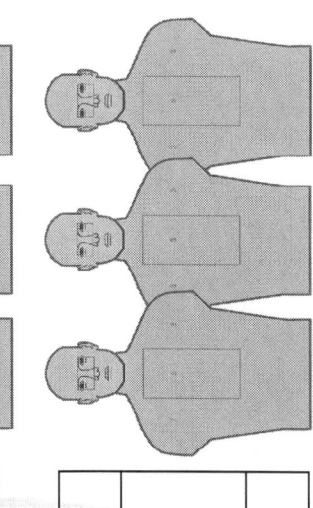
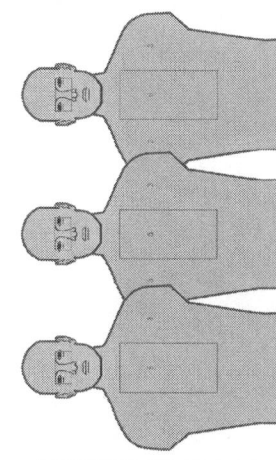

Date:	Location:	Rifle:	Scope / Micro Dot
Rep 1 Time:	Rep 2 Time:	Rep 3 Time:	Notes:
+ Penalties:	+ Penalties:	+ Penalties:	
= Rep 1 Score:	= Rep 2 Score:	= Rep 3 Score:	**Ave Rep Score:**

Date:	Location:	Rifle:	Scope / Micro Dot
Rep 1 Time:	Rep 2 Time:	Rep 3 Time:	Notes:
+ Penalties:	+ Penalties:	+ Penalties:	
= Rep 1 Score:	= Rep 2 Score:	= Rep 3 Score:	**Ave Rep Score:**

Date:	Location:	Rifle:	Scope / Micro Dot
Rep 1 Time:	Rep 2 Time:	Rep 3 Time:	Notes:
+ Penalties:	+ Penalties:	+ Penalties:	
= Rep 1 Score:	= Rep 2 Score:	= Rep 3 Score:	**Ave Rep Score:**

Precision Rifle ©

Gunfighter Drills - 3

ASSAULT COURSE

Purpose: Test all unsupported shooing positions.

Distance: 200, 150, 100 and 50 yards.

Target: JD-QUAL1

Par Time: 120 Seconds.

Extra Equipment Needed: Shot timer.

Total Rounds Fired: 8 Rounds.

Point Penalty: As per target score. 4 shots must be in the head and 4 shots must be in the body.

Starting Position & Condition: Standing low ready. 250 yards from target. Condition 1.

Description: At the timer beep, weapon on safe, in the low ready, move from 250 yard line quickly to the 200 yard line. Using any shooting position, aim and fire 2 rounds center mass of the body A box. Weapon on safe, in the low ready, move forward quickly to the 150 yard line. Using any shooting position, aim and fire 2 rounds center mass of the body A box. Weapon on safe, in the low ready, move forward quickly to the 100 yard line. Using any shooting position, aim and fire 2 rounds into the head A box. Weapon on safe, in the low ready, move forward quickly to the 50 yard line. Using any shooting position, aim and fire 2 rounds into the head A box. Record time and score.

Goals: Novice: 32 Points under par.   Expert: 40 Points under par.   Gunfighter: 40 Points with all rounds in head A box under par.

Variations: Try for all head A box.

ASSAULT COURSE

Date:	Rifle:	Scope:	Head / Body	Time:
200 Position:	150 Position:	100 Position:	50 Position:	**Total Score:**

Date:	Rifle:	Scope:	Head / Body	Time:
200 Position:	150 Position:	100 Position:	50 Position:	**Total Score:**

Date:	Rifle:	Scope:	Head / Body	Time:
200 Position:	150 Position:	100 Position:	50 Position:	**Total Score:**

Date:	Rifle:	Scope:	Head / Body	Time:
200 Position:	150 Position:	100 Position:	50 Position:	**Total Score:**

Date:	Rifle:	Scope:	Head / Body	Time:
200 Position:	150 Position:	100 Position:	50 Position:	**Total Score:**

Gunfighter Drills - 4

Precision Rifle ©

ASSAULT COURSE

www.GUNFIGHTERSERIES.com ©

Date:	Rifle:	Scope:	Head / Body	Time:
200 Position:	150 Position:	100 Position:	50 Position:	**Total Score:**

Date:	Rifle:	Scope:	Head / Body	Time:
200 Position:	150 Position:	100 Position:	50 Position:	**Total Score:**

Date:	Rifle:	Scope:	Head / Body	Time:
200 Position:	150 Position:	100 Position:	50 Position:	**Total Score:**

Date:	Rifle:	Scope:	Head / Body	Time:
200 Position:	150 Position:	100 Position:	50 Position:	**Total Score:**

Date:	Rifle:	Scope:	Head / Body	Time:
200 Position:	150 Position:	100 Position:	50 Position:	**Total Score:**

ASSAULT COURSE

Date:	Rifle:	Scope:	Head / Body	Time:
200 Position:	150 Position:	100 Position:	50 Position:	**Total Score:**

Date:	Rifle:	Scope:	Head / Body	Time:
200 Position:	150 Position:	100 Position:	50 Position:	**Total Score:**

Date:	Rifle:	Scope:	Head / Body	Time:
200 Position:	150 Position:	100 Position:	50 Position:	**Total Score:**

Date:	Rifle:	Scope:	Head / Body	Time:
200 Position:	150 Position:	100 Position:	50 Position:	**Total Score:**

Date:	Rifle:	Scope:	Head / Body	Time:
200 Position:	150 Position:	100 Position:	50 Position:	**Total Score:**

Gunfighter Drills - 4

Precision Rifle ©

ASSAULT COURSE

www.GUNFIGHTERSERIES.com ©

Date:	Rifle:	Scope:	Head / Body	Time:
200 Position:	150 Position:	100 Position:	50 Position:	**Total Score:**

Date:	Rifle:	Scope:	Head / Body	Time:
200 Position:	150 Position:	100 Position:	50 Position:	**Total Score:**

Date:	Rifle:	Scope:	Head / Body	Time:
200 Position:	150 Position:	100 Position:	50 Position:	**Total Score:**

Date:	Rifle:	Scope:	Head / Body	Time:
200 Position:	150 Position:	100 Position:	50 Position:	**Total Score:**

Date:	Rifle:	Scope:	Head / Body	Time:
200 Position:	150 Position:	100 Position:	50 Position:	**Total Score:**

ASSAULT COURSE

Date:	Rifle:	Scope:	Head / Body	Time:
200 Position:	150 Position:	100 Position:	50 Position:	**Total Score:**

Date:	Rifle:	Scope:	Head / Body	Time:
200 Position:	150 Position:	100 Position:	50 Position:	**Total Score:**

Date:	Rifle:	Scope:	Head / Body	Time:
200 Position:	150 Position:	100 Position:	50 Position:	**Total Score:**

Date:	Rifle:	Scope:	Head / Body	Time:
200 Position:	150 Position:	100 Position:	50 Position:	**Total Score:**

Date:	Rifle:	Scope:	Head / Body	Time:
200 Position:	150 Position:	100 Position:	50 Position:	**Total Score:**

Gunfighter Drills - 4

Precision Rifle ©

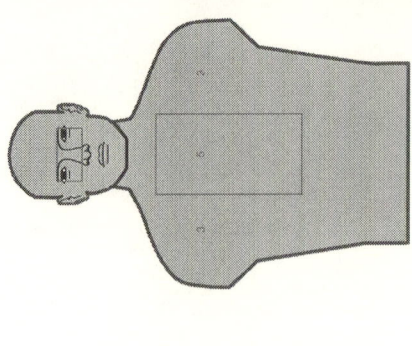

SNIPER SPRINTS

Purpose: Test getting in and out of unsupported shooing positions, reloads and accuracy while under stress.

Distance: 200, 175, 150, 125 and 100 yards.

Target: JD-QUAL1

Extra Equipment Needed: Shot timer. 3 Rifle mags with 5 rounds each.

Total Rounds Fired: 15 Rounds.

Point Penalty: Time plus penalty.

Starting Position & Condition: Standing low ready at 200 yard line. Condition 1.

Description: At the timer beep, engage the target center mass A Zone (5 point) body box from 200 yards with one round in the standing position. Put your weapon on safe, carry in the low ready and move forward quickly to the 175 yard line. Engage the target center mass A Zone (5 point) body box with one round in the standing position. Weapon on safe, low ready and move forward quickly to the 150 yard line. Engage the target center mass A Zone (5 point) body box with one round in the standing position. Weapon on safe, low ready and move forward quickly to the 125 yard line. Engage the target center mass A Zone (5 point) body box with one round in the standing position. Weapon on safe, low ready and move quickly to the 100 yard line. Engage the target center mass A Zone (5 point) body box with one round in the standing position.

Weapon goes dry. Weapon on safe, low ready, turn around and move quickly move back to the 200 yard line. Reload on the move (range rules dependent). You are still on the clock!

Continue the same drill in the kneeling and then again in the prone. For every hit in the 3 scoring zone, add 10 seconds to your time. For every hit in the 0 scoring zone, add 30 seconds to your time. Add the penalty time onto your recorded time for that repetition.

Goals: Beat your personal best time.

Variations: Head A box only.

SNIPER SPRINTS

Date:	Rifle:	Scope:	Ammo:	Notes:
Head / Body	Time:	Penalties:	**Total Score:**	

Date:	Rifle:	Scope:	Ammo:	Notes:
Head / Body	Time:	Penalties:	**Total Score:**	

Date:	Rifle:	Scope:	Ammo:	Notes:
Head / Body	Time:	Penalties:	**Total Score:**	

Date:	Rifle:	Scope:	Ammo:	Notes:
Head / Body	Time:	Penalties:	**Total Score:**	

Date:	Rifle:	Scope:	Ammo:	Notes:
Head / Body	Time:	Penalties:	**Total Score:**	

Precision Rifle ©

Gunfighter Drills - 5

SNIPER SPRINTS

Date:	Rifle:	Scope:	Ammo:	Notes:
	Time:	Penalties:	**Total Score:**	
Head / Body				

Date:	Rifle:	Scope:	Ammo:	Notes:
	Time:	Penalties:	**Total Score:**	
Head / Body				

Date:	Rifle:	Scope:	Ammo:	Notes:
	Time:	Penalties:	**Total Score:**	
Head / Body				

Date:	Rifle:	Scope:	Ammo:	Notes:
	Time:	Penalties:	**Total Score:**	
Head / Body				

Date:	Rifle:	Scope:	Ammo:	Notes:
	Time:	Penalties:	**Total Score:**	
Head / Body				

www.GUNFIGHTERSERIES.com ©

SNIPER SPRINTS

Date:	Rifle:	Scope:	Ammo:	Notes:
Head / Body	Time:	Penalties:	**Total Score:**	

Date:	Rifle:	Scope:	Ammo:	Notes:
Head / Body	Time:	Penalties:	**Total Score:**	

Date:	Rifle:	Scope:	Ammo:	Notes:
Head / Body	Time:	Penalties:	**Total Score:**	

Date:	Rifle:	Scope:	Ammo:	Notes:
Head / Body	Time:	Penalties:	**Total Score:**	

Date:	Rifle:	Scope:	Ammo:	Notes:
Head / Body	Time:	Penalties:	**Total Score:**	

Precision Rifle ©

SNIPER SPRINTS

www.GUNFIGHTERSERIES.com ©

Date:	Rifle:	Scope:	Ammo:	Notes:
Head / Body	Time:	Penalties:	**Total Score:**	

Date:	Rifle:	Scope:	Ammo:	Notes:
Head / Body	Time:	Penalties:	**Total Score:**	

Date:	Rifle:	Scope:	Ammo:	Notes:
Head / Body	Time:	Penalties:	**Total Score:**	

Date:	Rifle:	Scope:	Ammo:	Notes:
Head / Body	Time:	Penalties:	**Total Score:**	

Date:	Rifle:	Scope:	Ammo:	Notes:
Head / Body	Time:	Penalties:	**Total Score:**	

SNIPER SPRINTS

Date:		Rifle:	Scope:	Ammo:	Notes:
Head / Body		Time:	Penalties:	**Total Score:**	

Date:		Rifle:	Scope:	Ammo:	Notes:
Head / Body		Time:	Penalties:	**Total Score:**	

Date:		Rifle:	Scope:	Ammo:	Notes:
Head / Body		Time:	Penalties:	**Total Score:**	

Date:		Rifle:	Scope:	Ammo:	Notes:
Head / Body		Time:	Penalties:	**Total Score:**	

Date:		Rifle:	Scope:	Ammo:	Notes:
Head / Body		Time:	Penalties:	**Total Score:**	

Precision Rifle ©

Gunfighter Drills - 5

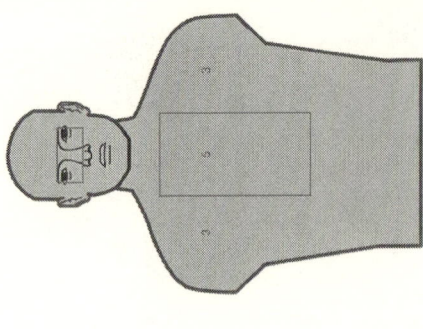

SNAP SHOT

Purpose: Close range immediate action defensive shooting.

Distance: 20 Yards.

Target: JD-QUAL1

Par Time: 2 Seconds.

Extra Equipment Needed: Shot timer.

Rounds Fired Per Rep: 1 Round.　　**Total Rounds Fired**: 5 Rounds.

Point Penalty: As per target score.

Repetitions: 5 Reps.

Starting Position & Condition: Standing low ready. Condition 1.

Description: At the timer beep, present your rifle to the threat and fire as soon as you acquire a flash sight picture of the A Zone (5 point) body or head box.

NOTE: It's best to patrol with your rifle scope on it's lowest power setting.

Goals: Novice: 20 points under par.　　Expert: 25 points under par.　　Gunfighter: 25 points with all rounds in head A box under par.

Variations: Start standing behind cover. On the buzzer take a large step left/right to clear cover then engage.

www.GUNFIGHTERSERIES.com ©

SNAP SHOT

Date:	Location:	Rifle:	Scope / Micro Dot	Power Setting:
Behind Cover: Y / N	A Zone: Body / Head	# In A Box:	# Over Par:	**Total Score:**

Date:	Location:	Rifle:	Scope / Micro Dot	Power Setting:
Behind Cover: Y / N	A Zone: Body / Head	# In A Box:	# Over Par:	**Total Score:**

Date:	Location:	Rifle:	Scope / Micro Dot	Power Setting:
Behind Cover: Y / N	A Zone: Body / Head	# In A Box:	# Over Par:	**Total Score:**

Date:	Location:	Rifle:	Scope / Micro Dot	Power Setting:
Behind Cover: Y / N	A Zone: Body / Head	# In A Box:	# Over Par:	**Total Score:**

Date:	Location:	Rifle:	Scope / Micro Dot	Power Setting:
Behind Cover: Y / N	A Zone: Body / Head	# In A Box:	# Over Par:	**Total Score:**

Gunfighter Drills - 6

Precision Rifle ©

SNAP SHOT

www.GUNFIGHTERSERIES.com ©

Date:	Location:	Rifle:	Scope / Micro Dot	Power Setting:
Behind Cover: Y / N	A Zone: Body / Head	# In A Box:	# Over Par:	Total Score:

Date:	Location:	Rifle:	Scope / Micro Dot	Power Setting:
Behind Cover: Y / N	A Zone: Body / Head	# In A Box:	# Over Par:	Total Score:

Date:	Location:	Rifle:	Scope / Micro Dot	Power Setting:
Behind Cover: Y / N	A Zone: Body / Head	# In A Box:	# Over Par:	Total Score:

Date:	Location:	Rifle:	Scope / Micro Dot	Power Setting:
Behind Cover: Y / N	A Zone: Body / Head	# In A Box:	# Over Par:	Total Score:

Date:	Location:	Rifle:	Scope / Micro Dot	Power Setting:
Behind Cover: Y / N	A Zone: Body / Head	# In A Box:	# Over Par:	Total Score:

SNAP SHOT

Date:	Location:	Rifle:	Scope / Micro Dot	Power Setting:
Behind Cover: Y / N	A Zone: Body / Head	# In A Box:	# Over Par:	**Total Score:**

Date:	Location:	Rifle:	Scope / Micro Dot	Power Setting:
Behind Cover: Y / N	A Zone: Body / Head	# In A Box:	# Over Par:	**Total Score:**

Date:	Location:	Rifle:	Scope / Micro Dot	Power Setting:
Behind Cover: Y / N	A Zone: Body / Head	# In A Box:	# Over Par:	**Total Score:**

Date:	Location:	Rifle:	Scope / Micro Dot	Power Setting:
Behind Cover: Y / N	A Zone: Body / Head	# n A Box:	# Over Par:	**Total Score:**

Date:	Location:	Rifle:	Scope / Micro Dot	Power Setting:
Behind Cover: Y / N	A Zone: Body / Head	# In A Box:	# Over Par:	**Total Score:**

Precision Rifle ©

SNAP SHOT

Date:	Location:	Rifle:	Scope / Micro Dot	Power Setting:
Behind Cover: Y / N	A Zone: Body / Head	# In A Box:	# Over Par:	Total Score:

Date:	Location:	Rifle:	Scope / Micro Dot	Power Setting:
Behind Cover: Y / N	A Zone: Body / Head	# In A Box:	# Over Par:	Total Score:

Date:	Location:	Rifle:	Scope / Micro Dot	Power Setting:
Behind Cover: Y / N	A Zone: Body / Head	# In A Box:	# Over Par:	Total Score:

Date:	Location:	Rifle:	Scope / Micro Dot	Power Setting:
Behind Cover: Y / N	A Zone: Body / Head	# In A Box:	# Over Par:	Total Score:

Date:	Location:	Rifle:	Scope / Micro Dot	Power Setting:
Behind Cover: Y / N	A Zone: Body / Head	# In A Box:	# Over Par:	Total Score:

www.GUNFIGHTERSERIES.com ©

SNAP SHOT

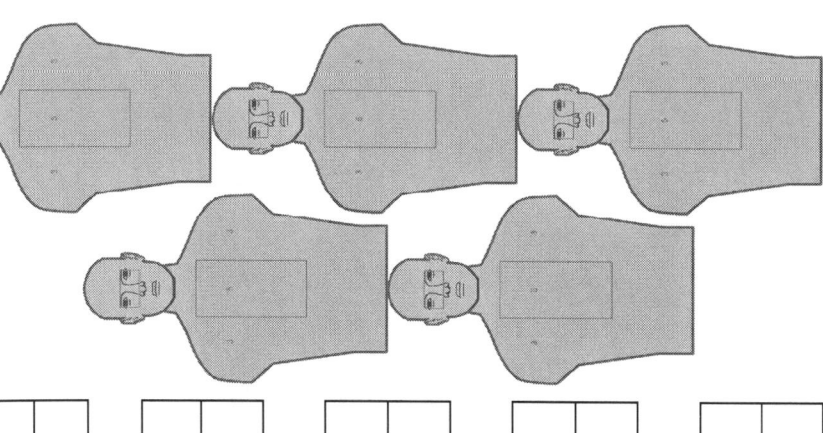

Date:	Location:	Rifle:	Scope / Micro Dot	Power Setting:
Behind Cover: Y / N	A Zone: Body / Head	# In A Box:	# Over Par:	**Total Score:**

Date:	Location:	Rifle:	Scope / Micro Dot	Power Setting:
Behind Cover: Y / N	A Zone: Body / Head	# In A Box:	# Over Par:	**Total Score:**

Date:	Location:	Rifle:	Scope / Micro Dot	Power Setting:
Behind Cover: Y / N	A Zone: Body / Head	# In A Box:	# Over Par:	**Total Score:**

Date:	Location:	Rifle:	Scope / Micro Dot	Power Setting:
Behind Cover: Y / N	A Zone: Body / Head	# In A Box:	# Over Par:	**Total Score:**

Date:	Location:	Rifle:	Scope / Micro Dot	Power Setting:
Behind Cover: Y / N	A Zone: Body / Head	# In A Box:	# Over Par:	**Total Score:**

Precision Rifle ©

Gunfighter Drills - 6

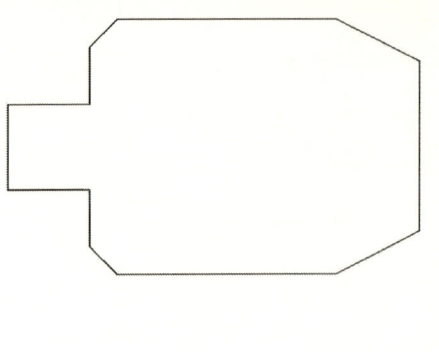

MOVEMENT TO CONTACT

Purpose: Familiarize and understanding point blank theory, elevated heart rate and close range defensive shooting.

Distance: 500, 450, 400, 350, 300, 250, 200, 150, 100, Yards.

Target: Full size steel silhouette target.

Extra Equipment Needed: Shot timer. Shooting partner with spotting scope. 9 barricades positions.

Total Rounds Fired: 9 Rounds.

Point Penalty: For every miss add 10 seconds to your time. For every hit in the body below the head add 2 seconds to your time.

Starting Position & Condition: Standing - low ready. Condition 1. Rifle set on 300 yard ZERO.

Description: Starting 500 yards away from the target. Rifle stays on 300 yard ZERO entire drill. At the timer beep, using provided cover and support, aim and fire 1 round center mass. Weapon on safe, in the low ready, move quickly to the 450 yard line. Using provided cover and support, aim and fire 1 round center mass. Weapon on safe, in the low ready, move quickly to the 400 yard line. Continue until you fire the last round at 100 yards. Record time and score. Add the penalty time onto your recorded time for that repetition.

Note: Do not time the 1st attempt at this drill; the purpose of this drill is to understand that most precision rifle calibers can score hits on man sized target from 0-500 yards using a 300 yard ZERO. Some ballistic calculators have "point blank" features for custom target dimensions. Do this drill once then begin to use your close/mid range hold over/unders to tighten groups in the head portion of the target.

Goals: Beat your personal best time.

MOVEMENT TO CONTACT

Date:	Location:	Rifle:	Scope:	Notes:
Total Time:	Score:	Penalties:	**Total Time Score:**	

Date:	Location:	Rifle:	Scope:	Notes:
Total Time:	Score:	Penalties:	**Total Time Score:**	

Date:	Location:	Rifle:	Scope:	Notes:
Total Time:	Score:	Penalties:	**Total Time Score:**	

Date:	Location:	Rifle:	Scope:	Notes:
Total Time:	Score:	Penalties:	**Total Time Score:**	

Date:	Location:	Rifle:	Scope:	Notes:
Total Time:	Score:	Penalties:	**Total Time Score:**	

Gunfighter Drills - 7

Precision Rifle ©

MOVEMENT TO CONTACT

www.GUNFIGHTERSERIES.com ©

Date:	Location:	Rifle:	Scope:	Notes:
Total Time:	Score:	Penalties:	Total Time Score:	

Date:	Location:	Rifle:	Scope:	Notes:
Total Time:	Score:	Penalties:	Total Time Score:	

Date:	Location:	Rifle:	Scope:	Notes:
Total Time:	Score:	Penalties:	Total Time Score:	

Date:	Location:	Rifle:	Scope:	Notes:
Total Time:	Score:	Penalties:	Total Time Score:	

Date:	Location:	Rifle:	Scope:	Notes:
Total Time:	Score:	Penalties:	Total Time Score:	

MOVEMENT TO CONTACT

Date:	Location:	Rifle:	Scope:	Notes:
Total Time:	Score:	Penalties:	**Total Time Score:**	

Date:	Location:	Rifle:	Scope:	Notes:
Total Time:	Score:	Penalties:	**Total Time Score:**	

Date:	Location:	Rifle:	Scope:	Notes:
Total Time:	Score:	Penalties:	**Total Time Score:**	

Date:	Location:	Rifle:	Scope:	Notes:
Total Time:	Score:	Penalties:	**Total Time Score:**	

Date:	Location:	Rifle:	Scope:	Notes:
Total Time:	Score:	Penalties:	**Total Time Score:**	

MOVEMENT TO CONTACT

Date:	Location:	Rifle:	Scope:	Notes:
Total Time:	Score:	Penalties:	**Total Time Score:**	

Date:	Location:	Rifle:	Scope:	Notes:
Total Time:	Score:	Penalties:	**Total Time Score:**	

Date:	Location:	Rifle:	Scope:	Notes:
Total Time:	Score:	Penalties:	**Total Time Score:**	

Date:	Location:	Rifle:	Scope:	Notes:
Total Time:	Score:	Penalties:	**Total Time Score:**	

Date:	Location:	Rifle:	Scope:	Notes:
Total Time:	Score:	Penalties:	**Total Time Score:**	

www.GUNFIGHTERSERIES.com ©

MOVEMENT TO CONTACT

Date:	Location:	Rifle:	Scope:	Notes:
Total Time:	Score:	Penalties:	Total Time Score:	

Date:	Location:	Rifle:	Scope:	Notes:
Total Time:	Score:	Penalties:	Total Time Score:	

Date:	Location:	Rifle:	Scope:	Notes:
Total Time:	Score:	Penalties:	Total Time Score:	

Date:	Location:	Rifle:	Scope:	Notes:
Total Time:	Score:	Penalties:	Total Time Score:	

Date:	Location:	Rifle:	Scope:	Notes:
Total Time:	Score:	Penalties:	Total Time Score:	

Gunfighter Drills - 7

Precision Rifle ©

BREAK CONTACT

Purpose: Close range defensive shooting.

Distance: 10, 20, 50, 75, 100, 125 and 150 Yards.

Target: JD-QUAL1

Extra Equipment Needed: Shot timer. Pistol, 1 mag with 5 rounds and holster. 1 Rifle mag with 5 rounds. 6 barricades positions.

Total Rounds Fired: 5 Pistol & 5 rifle rounds.

Point Penalty: Time plus penalty. (1 Shot in head A box. 9 Shots in body A box.)

Starting Position & Condition: Standing - Surrender / Interview. Pistol holstered in condition 1. Rifle slung across back. Condition 3.

Description: Starting 10 yards from the target, at the timer beep, draw your pistol and fire 2 rounds to the body A box and 1 round into head a box. Weapon on safe, in the low or high ready, turn around and move to the 20 yard line. Turn down range then engage 2 rounds to the body A box. Holster empty pistol and safely unsling rifle.

With your rifle on safe, in the low ready, turn around and move up range to the 50 yard line. Turn down range, from any shooting position engage 1 rounds to the body A box. Continue the drill using any shooting position and aiming at body A box until completed at 150 yards.

Record time and score the target. For every hit in the 3 scoring zone, add 10 seconds to your time. For every hit in the 0 scoring zone, add 30 seconds to your time. Add the penalty time onto your recorded time for that repetition. Average all of the repetitions and there is your time.

Goals: Novice: 180 Seconds.   Expert: 100 Seconds.   Gunfighter: 60 Seconds.

Variation: Head shots only.

BREAK CONTACT

Date:	Location:	Rifle:	Scope:	Pistol:
Total Time:	# of Head A:	# of Body A:	Penalties:	**Total Time Score:**

Date:	Location:	Rifle:	Scope:	Pistol:
Total Time:	# of Head A:	# of Body A:	Penalties:	**Total Time Score:**

Date:	Location:	Rifle:	Scope:	Pistol:
Total Time:	# of Head A:	# of Body A:	Penalties:	**Total Time Score:**

Date:	Location:	Rifle:	Scope:	Pistol:
Total Time:	# of Head A:	# of Body A:	Penalties:	**Total Time Score:**

Date:	Location:	Rifle:	Scope:	Pistol:
Total Time:	# of Head A:	# of Body A:	Penalties:	**Total Time Score:**

Precision Rifle ©

BREAK CONTACT

Date:	Location:	Rifle:	Scope:	Pistol:
Total Time:	# of Head A:	# of Body A:	Penalties:	**Total Time Score:**

Date:	Location:	Rifle:	Scope:	Pistol:
Total Time:	# of Head A:	# of Body A:	Penalties:	**Total Time Score:**

Date:	Location:	Rifle:	Scope:	Pistol:
Total Time:	# of Head A:	# of Body A:	Penalties:	**Total Time Score:**

Date:	Location:	Rifle:	Scope:	Pistol:
Total Time:	# of Head A:	# of Body A:	Penalties:	**Total Time Score:**

Date:	Location:	Rifle:	Scope:	Pistol:
Total Time:	# of Head A:	# of Body A:	Penalties:	**Total Time Score:**

www.GUNFIGHTERSERIES.com ©

BREAK CONTACT

Date:	Location:	Rifle:	Scope:	Pistol:
Total Time:	# of Head A:	# of Body A:	Penalties:	**Total Time Score:**

Date:	Location:	Rifle:	Scope:	Pistol:
Total Time:	# of Head A:	# of Body A:	Penalties:	**Total Time Score:**

Date:	Location:	Rifle:	Scope:	Pistol:
Total Time:	# of Head A:	# of Body A:	Penalties:	**Total Time Score:**

Date:	Location:	Rifle:	Scope:	Pistol:
Total Time:	# of Head A:	# of Body A:	Penalties:	**Total Time Score:**

Date:	Location:	Rifle:	Scope:	Pistol:
Total Time:	# of Head A:	# of Body A:	Penalties:	**Total Time Score:**

BREAK CONTACT

Date:	Location:	Rifle:	Scope:	Pistol:
Total Time:	# of Head A:	# of Body A:	Penalties:	**Total Time Score:**

Date:	Location:	Rifle:	Scope:	Pistol:
Total Time:	# of Head A:	# of Body A:	Penalties:	**Total Time Score:**

Date:	Location:	Rifle:	Scope:	Pistol:
Total Time:	# of Head A:	# of Body A:	Penalties:	**Total Time Score:**

Date:	Location:	Rifle:	Scope:	Pistol:
Total Time:	# of Head A:	# of Body A:	Penalties:	**Total Time Score:**

Date:	Location:	Rifle:	Scope:	Pistol:
Total Time:	# of Head A:	# of Body A:	Penalties:	**Total Time Score:**

www.GUNFIGHTERSERIES.com ©

BREAK CONTACT

Date:	Location:	Rifle:	Scope:	Pistol:
Total Time:	# of Head A:	# of Body A:	Penalties:	**Total Time Score:**

Date:	Location:	Rifle:	Scope:	Pistol:
Total Time:	# of Head A:	# of Body A:	Penalties:	**Total Time Score:**

Date:	Location:	Rifle:	Scope:	Pistol:
Total Time:	# of Head A:	# of Body A:	Penalties:	**Total Time Score:**

Date:	Location:	Rifle:	Scope:	Pistol:
Total Time:	# of Head A:	# of Body A:	Penalties:	**Total Time Score:**

Date:	Location:	Rifle:	Scope:	Pistol:
Total Time:	# of Head A:	# of Body A:	Penalties:	**Total Time Score:**

Gunfighter Drills - 8

Precision Rifle ©

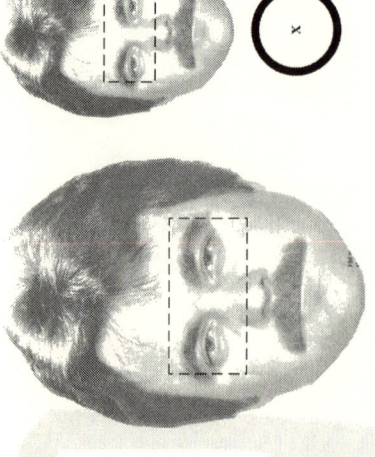

FBI SNIPER QUAL

- **Ammo**: 10 Rounds total.
- **Target**: Big head, small head, 2 inch circle.
- **Distance**: 100 yards.
- **Scoring**: Cold bore shot is pass / fail. Passing score is 90 points.
- **Starting Position & Condition**: Rifle on the firing line. Standing behind rifle to prone. Condition 4.

Stage	#Rnds	Time	Position/Description
1	1	60 Sec	Standing to prone. 1 round into A box of the big head target. Pass / Fail
2	2	120 Sec	Standing to prone. 2 rounds into A box of the small head target.

4 Minute jog to elevate heart rate.

| 3 | 3 | 70 Sec | Standing to prone. 3 rounds into A box of the big head target. |
| 4 | 4 | 120 Sec | Standing to prone. 4 rounds into the 2 inch circle target. |

www.GUNFIGHTERSERIES.com ©

FBI SNIPER QUAL

Date:		Time:		Temp:	Baro:
Rifle:		Scope:		Ammo:	
Stage 1: Cold Bore	Make time: Y / N			Pass 10 Points / Fail	
Stage 2: 200 Yard Simulation	Make time: Y / N			Score out of 20:	
Stage 3: Elevated Heart Rate	Make time: Y / N			Score out of 30:	
Stage 4: Rapid Fire	Make time: Y / N			Score out of 40:	
Notes:				**Total Score:**	

Date:		Time:		Temp:	Baro:
Rifle:		Scope:		Ammo:	
Stage 1: Cold Bore	Make time: Y / N			Pass 10 Points / Fail	
Stage 2: 200 Yard Simulation	Make time: Y / N			Score out of 20:	
Stage 3: Elevated Heart Rate	Make time: Y / N			Score out of 30:	
Stage 4: Rapid Fire	Make time: Y / N			Score out of 40:	
Notes:				**Total Score:**	

Qualification COF - 1

Precision Rifle ©

FBI SNIPER QUAL

Date:	Time:	Temp:	Baro:
Rifle:	Scope:	Ammo:	
Stage 1: Cold Bore	Make time: Y / N	Pass 10 Points / Fail	
Stage 2: 200 Yard Simulation	Make time: Y / N	Score out of 20:	
Stage 3: Elevated Heart Rate	Make time: Y / N	Score out of 30:	
Stage 4: Rapid Fire	Make time: Y / N	Score out of 40:	
Notes:		**Total Score:**	

Date:	Time:	Temp:	Baro:
Rifle:	Scope:	Ammo:	
Stage 1: Cold Bore	Make time: Y / N	Pass 10 Points / Fail	
Stage 2: 200 Yard Simulation	Make time: Y / N	Score out of 20:	
Stage 3: Elevated Heart Rate	Make time: Y / N	Score out of 30:	
Stage 4: Rapid Fire	Make time: Y / N	Score out of 40:	
Notes:		**Total Score:**	

FBI SNIPER QUAL

Date:	Time:	Temp:	Baro:
Rifle:	Scope:	Ammo:	
Stage 1: Cold Bore	Make time: Y / N		Pass 10 Points / Fail
Stage 2: 200 Yard Simulation	Make time: Y / N	Score out of 20:	
Stage 3: Elevated Heart Rate	Make time: Y / N	Score out of 30:	
Stage 4: Rapid Fire	Make time: Y / N	Score out of 40:	
Notes:		**Total Score:**	

Date:	Time:	Temp:	Baro:
Rifle:	Scope:	Ammo:	
Stage 1: Cold Bore	Make time: Y / N		Pass 10 Points / Fail
Stage 2: 200 Yard Simulation	Make time: Y / N	Score out of 20:	
Stage 3: Elevated Heart Rate	Make time: Y / N	Score out of 30:	
Stage 4: Rapid Fire	Make time: Y / N	Score out of 40:	
Notes:		**Total Score:**	

Qualification COF - 1

Precision Rifle ©

FBI SNIPER QUAL

Date:	Time:	Temp:	Baro:
Rifle:	Scope:	Ammo:	Pass 10 Points / Fail
Stage 1: Cold Bore	Make time: Y / N		
Stage 2: 200 Yard Simulation	Make time: Y / N	Score out of 20:	
Stage 3: Elevated Heart Rate	Make time: Y / N	Score out of 30:	
Stage 4: Rapid Fire	Make time: Y / N	Score out of 40:	
Notes:		**Total Score:**	

Date:	Time:	Temp:	Baro:
Rifle:	Scope:	Ammo:	Pass 10 Points / Fail
Stage 1: Cold Bore	Make time: Y / N		
Stage 2: 200 Yard Simulation	Make time: Y / N	Score out of 20:	
Stage 3: Elevated Heart Rate	Make time: Y / N	Score out of 30:	
Stage 4: Rapid Fire	Make time: Y / N	Score out of 40:	
Notes:		**Total Score:**	

FBI SNIPER QUAL

Date:	Time:	Temp:	Baro:
Rifle:	Scope:	Ammo:	
Stage 1: Cold Bore	Make time: Y / N	Pass 10 Points / Fail	
Stage 2: 200 Yard Simulation	Make time: Y / N	Score out of 20:	
Stage 3: Elevated Heart Rate	Make time: Y / N	Score out of 30:	
Stage 4: Rapid Fire	Make time: Y / N	Score out of 40:	
Notes:		**Total Score:**	

Date:	Time:	Temp:	Baro:
Rifle:	Scope:	Ammo:	
Stage 1: Cold Bore	Make time: Y / N	Pass 10 Points / Fail	
Stage 2: 200 Yard Simulation	Make time: Y / N	Score out of 20:	
Stage 3: Elevated Heart Rate	Make time: Y / N	Score out of 30:	
Stage 4: Rapid Fire	Make time: Y / N	Score out of 40:	
Notes:		**Total Score:**	

Precision Rifle ©

Qualification COF - 1

www.GUNFIGHTERSERIES.com ©

GUNFIGHTER PRECISION RIFLE STANDARD 1

- **Ammo**: 25 Rounds total. 2 Magazines needed.
- **Target**: JD-QUAL1 X 3. Stage 6: Spread targets apart horizontally, as far as possible. Stage 7: Spread targets apart over a 250 yard area.
- **Scoring**: As per target score. Subtract 5 points for any shot over time. Passing score is 100 out of 125 points.
- **Starting Position & Condition**: All stages start with rifle on the firing line on personal ZERO and standing behind rifle (unless noted). Condition 4.

Stage	Distance	#Rnds	Time	Position/Description
1	UKD 50 - 150 Yards	1	90 Sec	Using a non prone, supported shooting position of choice, 1 round to HEAD A box.
2	100 Yards	1+1	45 Sec	Standing low ready to prone unsupported. 1 round to HEAD A box, reload, 1 round to BODY A box.
3	100 Yards	1+1	45 Sec	Standing low ready to kneeling unsupported. 1 round to HEAD A box, reload, 1 round to BODY A box.
4	100 Yards	1+1	45 Sec	Kneeling low ready to standing unsupported. 1 round to HEAD A box, reload, 1 round to BODY A box.
5	300 Yards	2+2+2	75 Sec	2 Rounds prone, 2 rounds kneeling and 2 rounds standing into BODY A box. (Supported)

Stage 6: Spread 3 targets apart horizontally, as far as possible all at 400 yards.

6	400 Yards X3 Targets	2+2+2	60 Sec	2 Rounds prone to BODY A box of each target. (Supported)

Stage 7: Spread 3 targets apart over a 250 yard area (between 500 to 750 yards).

7	UKD 500 - 750 yards X3 Targets	2+2+2	5 Min	Range estimate, calculate elevation and windage, engage with 2 rounds prone to BODY A box of each target a 3 different distance. (Supported)

GUNFIGHTER PRECISION RIFLE STANDARD 1

Date:	Time:		Location:	
Rifle:	Scope:		Ammo:	
Stage 1: 90 Sec = 1 Round	Under Par Time: Y / N	Sec.	Score:	(HEAD ONLY)
Stage 2: 45 Sec = 1 + 1 Rounds	Under Par Time: Y / N	Sec.	Score:	(HEAD + BODY)
Stage 3: 45 Sec = 1 + 1 Rounds	Under Par Time: Y / N	Sec.	Score:	(HEAD + BODY)
Stage 4: 45 Sec = 1 + 1 Rounds	Under Par Time: Y / N	Sec.	Score:	(HEAD + BODY)
Stage 5: 75 Sec = 2 + 2 + 2 Rounds	Under Par Time: Y / N	Sec.	Score:	(BODY ONLY)
Stage 6: 60 Sec = 2 + 2 + 2 Rounds	Under Par Time: Y / N	Sec.	Score:	(BODY ONLY)
Stage 7: 5 Min = 2 + 2 + 2 Rounds	Under Par Time: Y / N	Min.	Score:	(BODY ONLY)
Notes:			**Total Score:**	

Precision Rifle ©

Qualification COF - 2

GUNFIGHTER PRECISION RIFLE STANDARD 1

Date:	Time:	Location:
Rifle:	Scope:	Ammo:
Stage 1: 90 Sec = 1 Round	Under Par Time: Y / N Sec.	Score: (HEAD ONLY)
Stage 2: 45 Sec = 1 + 1 Rounds	Under Par Time: Y / N Sec.	Score: (HEAD + BODY)
Stage 3: 45 Sec = 1 + 1 Rounds	Under Par Time: Y / N Sec.	Score: (HEAD + BODY)
Stage 4: 45 Sec = 1 + 1 Rounds	Under Par Time: Y / N Sec.	Score: (HEAD + BODY)
Stage 5: 75 Sec = 2 + 2 + 2 Rounds	Under Par Time: Y / N Sec.	Score: (BODY ONLY)
Stage 6: 60 Sec = 2 + 2 + 2 Rounds	Under Par Time: Y / N Sec.	Score: (BODY ONLY)
Stage 7: 5 Min = 2 + 2 + 2 Rounds	Under Par Time: Y / N Min.	Score: (BODY ONLY)
Notes:		**Total Score:**

www.GUNFIGHTERSERIES.com ©

GUNFIGHTER PRECISION RIFLE STANDARD 1

Date:	Time:	Location:
Rifle:	Scope:	Ammo:
Stage 1: 90 Sec = 1 Round	Under Par Time: Y / N	Sec.	Score: (HEAD ONLY)
Stage 2: 45 Sec = 1 + 1 Rounds	Under Par Time: Y / N	Sec.	Score: (HEAD + BODY)
Stage 3: 45 Sec = 1 + 1 Rounds	Under Par Time: Y / N	Sec.	Score: (HEAD + BODY)
Stage 4: 45 Sec = 1 + 1 Rounds	Under Par Time: Y / N	Sec.	Score: (HEAD + BODY)
Stage 5: 75 Sec = 2 + 2 + 2 Rounds	Under Par Time: Y / N	Sec.	Score: (BODY ONLY)
Stage 6: 60 Sec = 2 + 2 + 2 Rounds	Under Par Time: Y / N	Sec.	Score: (BODY ONLY)
Stage 7: 5 Min = 2 + 2 + 2 Rounds	Under Par Time: Y / N	Min.	Score: (BODY ONLY)
Notes:			**Total Score:**

Qualification COF - 2

Precision Rifle ©

GUNFIGHTER PRECISION RIFLE STANDARD 1

Date:	Time:	Location:
Rifle:	Scope:	Ammo:
Stage 1: 90 Sec = 1 Round	Under Par Time: Y / N Sec.	Score: (HEAD ONLY)
Stage 2: 45 Sec = 1 + 1 Rounds	Under Par Time: Y / N Sec.	Score: (HEAD + BODY)
Stage 3: 45 Sec = 1 + 1 Rounds	Under Par Time: Y / N Sec.	Score: (HEAD + BODY)
Stage 4: 45 Sec = 1 + 1 Rounds	Under Par Time: Y / N Sec.	Score: (HEAD + BODY)
Stage 5: 75 Sec = 2 + 2 + 2 Rounds	Under Par Time: Y / N Sec.	Score: (BODY ONLY)
Stage 6: 60 Sec = 2 + 2 + 2 Rounds	Under Par Time: Y / N Sec.	Score: (BODY ONLY)
Stage 7: 5 Min = 2 + 2 + 2 Rounds	Under Par Time: Y / N Min.	Score: (BODY ONLY)
Notes:		**Total Score:**

GUNFIGHTER PRECISION RIFLE STANDARD 1

Date:	Time:	Location:
Rifle:	Scope:	Ammo:
Stage 1: 90 Sec = 1 Round	Under Par Time: Y / N	Sec.	Score: (HEAD ONLY)
Stage 2: 45 Sec = 1 + 1 Rounds	Under Par Time: Y / N	Sec.	Score: (HEAD + BODY)
Stage 3: 45 Sec = 1 + 1 Rounds	Under Par Time: Y / N	Sec.	Score: (HEAD + BODY)
Stage 4: 45 Sec = 1 + 1 Rounds	Under Par Time: Y / N	Sec.	Score: (HEAD + BODY)
Stage 5: 75 Sec = 2 + 2 + 2 Rounds	Under Par Time: Y / N	Sec.	Score: (BODY ONLY)
Stage 6: 60 Sec = 2 + 2 + 2 Rounds	Under Par Time: Y / N	Sec.	Score: (BODY ONLY)
Stage 7: 5 Min = 2 + 2 + 2 Rounds	Under Par Time: Y / N	Min.	Score: (BODY ONLY)
Notes:		**Total Score:**

Qualification COF - 2

Precision Rifle ©

www.GUNFIGHTERSERIES.com ©

NAME OF CUSTOM DRILL:

Purpose:

By:

Distance: Yards

Target:

Par Time: Seconds

Extra Equipment Needed:

Rounds per Repetition: Rounds

Total Rounds Fired: Rounds

Point Penalty:

Repetitions:

Starting Position & Condition: Start in the

Description:

Goals: Novice: Expert: Gunfighter:

Variations:

Custom Drill Name:

Date:	Location:	Weapon:	Sights:	Ammo
				Notes:
Date:	Location:	Weapon:	Sights:	Ammo
				Notes:
Date:	Location:	Weapon:	Sights:	Ammo
				Notes:
Date:	Location:	Weapon:	Sights:	Ammo
				Notes:
Date:	Location:	Weapon:	Sights:	Ammo
				Notes:

Custom Drill Name:

www.GUNFIGHTERSERIES.com ©

Date:	Location:	Weapon:	Sights:	Ammo
				Notes:
Date:	Location:	Weapon:	Sights:	Ammo
				Notes:
Date:	Location:	Weapon:	Sights:	Ammo
				Notes:
Date:	Location:	Weapon:	Sights:	Ammo
				Notes:
Date:	Location:	Weapon:	Sights:	Ammo
				Notes:

Custom Drill Name:

Date:	Location:	Weapon:	Sights:	Ammo
				Notes:
Date:	Location:	Weapon:	Sights:	Ammo
				Notes:
Date:	Location:	Weapon:	Sights:	Ammo
				Notes:
Date:	Location:	Weapon:	Sights:	Ammo
				Notes:
Date:	Location:	Weapon:	Sights:	Ammo
				Notes:

NOTES:

www.GUNFIGHTERSERIES.com ©

NOTES:

Training Classes Taken

Date:	Institute:	Class Name:	Weapon:
Notes about subjects covered:			
Notes about equipment used:			
Instructors Name:		Contact Info:	
Instructors Name:		Contact Info:	
Students Name:		Contact Info:	
Students Name:		Contact Info:	
Students Name:		Contact Info:	
Students Name:		Contact Info:	
Students Name:		Contact Info:	

www.GUNFIGHTERSERIES.com ©

Training Classes Taken

| Date: | Institute: | Class Name: | Weapon: |

Notes about subjects covered:

_____
_____
_____
_____

Notes about equipment used:

_____
_____
_____
_____

Instructors Name: _____ Contact Info: _____
Instructors Name: _____ Contact Info: _____
Students Name: _____ Contact Info: _____
Students Name: _____ Contact Info: _____
Students Name: _____ Contact Info: _____
Students Name: _____ Contact Info: _____
Students Name: _____ Contact Info: _____

Training Classes Taken

Date:	Institute:	Class Name:	Weapon:

Notes about subjects covered:

Notes about equipment used:

Instructors Name: Contact Info:

Instructors Name: Contact Info:

Students Name: Contact Info:

Students Name: Contact Info:

Students Name: Contact Info:

Students Name: Contact Info:

Students Name: Contact Info:

www.GUNFIGHTERSERIES.com ©

Training Classes Taken

Date:	Institute:	Class Name:	Weapon:

Notes about subjects covered:

_____
_____
_____
_____
_____

Notes about equipment used:

_____
_____
_____
_____
_____

Instructors Name: _____ Contact Info: _____

Instructors Name: _____ Contact Info: _____

Students Name: _____ Contact Info: _____

Students Name: _____ Contact Info: _____

Students Name: _____ Contact Info: _____

Students Name: _____ Contact Info: _____

Students Name: _____ Contact Info: _____

Training Classes Taken

Date:	Institute:	Class Name:	Weapon:

Notes about subjects covered:

Notes about equipment used:

Instructors Name: Contact Info:

Instructors Name: Contact Info:

Students Name: Contact Info:

Students Name: Contact Info:

Students Name: Contact Info:

Students Name: Contact Info:

Students Name: Contact Info:

www.GUNFIGHTERSERIES.com ©

Made in the USA
Middletown, DE
13 May 2021